A Changing Scene

$10.45   4/83

A Changing Scene

LUCETTE ROLLET KENAN

HARCOURT BRACE JOVANOVICH, INC.

NEW YORK   SAN DIEGO   CHICAGO   SAN FRANCISCO   ATLANTA
LONDON   SYDNEY   TORONTO

ISBN: 0-15-505900-9

Library of Congress Catalog Card Number: 81-82740

Printed in the United States of America

ILLUSTRATION CREDITS

All pictorial glosses are by Terry K. Schwarz. P. 1, © Georg Gerster—Rapho/Photo Researchers; 14, 15, © 1976 Christa Armstrong—Rapho/Photo Researchers; 26, 27, © Bettye Lane; 40, 41, 45, 52, NASA; 56, American Red Cross in Greater New York; 57, HBJ Photo; 70, 71, Hazel Hankin; 78, Marineland; 83, Springer/Bettmann Film Archive; 96, The Bettmann Archive; 97, © Bettye Lane; 109, Wide World Photos; 122, Burt Glinn/© Magnum Photos; 137, © 1976 Elizabeth Hamlin, Stock, Boston; 150, 164, HBJ Photo; Hazel Hankin; 165, Ben Lyon/Monterey Peninsula Herald; 167, HBJ Photo; 178 left, Hart Shaffner & Marx; 178 right, courtesy Levi Straus Co.; 179 left, Du Pont Company; 179 right, Courtesy Levi Straus Co., 191, Rose Skytta/Jeroboam, Inc.; 204, Eileen Christelow/Jeroboam, Inc.; Jeremiah Lighter; 205, © 1976 Smithsonian Institution; 220, HBJ Photo; 221, Barbara Paup, Jeroboam, Inc.; 234, Hazel Hankin; 235, Consolidated Edison Company
Cover photo; © Georg Gerster—Rapho/Photo Researchers

This book is dedicated to
William A. Pullin

PREFACE

A Changing Scene was composed with the double purpose of helping students of English as a second language to improve their skills in reading and in expressing themselves clearly, both orally and in writing. By the time they reach the end of this reader, students should have (1) increased their familiarity with English grammar, vocabulary, and idioms; (2) learned to recognize the main points of a story and to follow patterns of Western logical reasoning; (3) gained confidence in expressing their opinions in classroom discussions; (4) discovered aspects of American life that they may not have known, and compared them with the customs and values of other countries.

A special effort has been made to keep each chapter interesting from beginning to end by providing exercises that are appealing and entertaining. Many of the exercises tell stories related to the main theme and offer additional information or a different point of view. Whenever possible, the exercises allow students to use the grammar under study in a creative way, with a certain amount of freedom—almost as they would use it in conversation.

A Changing Scene consists of sixteen original articles and two pieces adapted from newspapers, one by Ann Landers, the other by foreign correspondent Fernand Auberjonois. The essays cover a wide variety of subjects, including, for instance, the joys and pains of mass tourism, family relationships, volunteer work, vandals, science fiction, working women, creative justice, the new role of the zoo, the problems of nuclear energy, and the do's and don'ts of job hunting. Although each reading is based on an aspect of life in the United States or a change in the values of American society, the topics were chosen for their universal appeal. The title of the book refers both to the changes occurring in modern society and to the variety of subjects presented.

The essays are arranged in order of increasing difficulty. The vocabulary reaches the 3,500 word-level of the New Horizon Ladder Dictionary; all words and expressions above that level are glossed or illustrated. Each article is followed by a comprehensive vocabulary section that integrates in a logical text all the new words, and many familiar ones, related to the theme of the article. Idioms and expressions, marked in the text with an asterisk, are carefully explained in a separate section.

The book makes full use of the power of repetition. Vocabulary, idioms, and grammatical constructions are used over and over throughout the eighteen chapters, and a word learned in the first article may reappear in the synonym exercise of a later chapter. Instructors will also find that more than one exercise may be devoted to a difficult question, such as the use of past tenses, relative pronouns, indirect speech, or the conditional tense.

The articles are written in the kind of everyday English that students encounter in newspapers and magazines. They should be read for their content without an attempt to understand every word or to analyze every structure. Two types of exercises, Understanding the Text and True or False?, allow instructors and students to make sure that the story has been fully understood and its main ideas recognized. The answers need not be long, but students should certainly be encouraged to give as much explanation as they wish; or they can simply refer to the part of the text that justifies their answers. The true-false exercises can be answered not only with a "yes" or a "no" but with another response when the statement is only partly true, for the purpose here is to make readers pay close attention to the text and meet the exercise with an alert mind. In Chapter 1, for example, the first true-false statement, "Traveling and tourism are modern activities," should bring a response like, "Tourism is a modern activity; traveling is not."

Although most of the exercises are meant to be done orally, they can be used for written work if preferred. Those that tell a story or add new facts to the information provided by the article may need two readings—one to do the required work and the other to concentrate on the content.

The object of the Vocabulary, Synonyms, and Idioms exercises is to help students master the new words and expressions introduced in each chapter, while the Word Forms exercises expand vocabulary by presenting, always in the same order, the nouns, verbs, adjectives, and adverbs from the same word family. Special exercises also provide practice in the use of articles and prepositions. A number of oral sentence-combining exercises appear throughout the book, but one particular kind, Combining Sentences, should be done in writing or prepared in writing before being repeated orally. This exercise allows students to use all the ways they know (and perhaps do not realize they know) of indicating the relationship between the various ideas in a sentence or group of sentences: the use of relative pronouns, gerund phrases, and such words as *and, but, for, however, since, although, because, when,* and *where,* which are the tools of logical reasoning.

By the time students reach the Topics for Discussion at the end of each chapter, they will have collected a great deal of information from the readings and exercises, and enough vocabulary to discuss the subject matter. These topics are meant to give students a chance to apply their newly acquired knowledge and to express their opinions about the articles and the issues they raise. The whole class should participate in the discussion, and students should be encouraged to support or criticize one another's views rather than address their comments to the instructor. Each chapter ends with a few simpler topics, For Composition Only, calling for the writing of outlines, summaries, or short personal essays.

I would like to express my gratitude to Shirley W. Braun of Rockefeller University in New York for her encouragement and her very constructive comments. My special thanks also to Len Fox of Brooklyn College and Teresa Dalle of Memphis State University for their excellent suggestions. All my thanks to Chris Pearson, Jeremiah Lighter, and Richard Lewis of Harcourt Brace Jovanovich, responsible for the production and design of the book; last but not least, I want to thank Lisa Haugaard, who guided me patiently and judiciously through the final editing stages of the book.

LUCETTE ROLLET KENAN

CONTENTS

A
Changing
Scene

Travelers and Tourists 1

FOR THOUSANDS of years men have been wandering around—for pleasure, for profit, or to satisfy their curiosity. When the only means of transportation° were horses, camels, and small boats, travelers were already crossing seas and deserts to acquire rare goods or to visit famous places. For the pure joy of learning, scholars° ventured into distant kingdoms and observed their customs. They tasted the foods; they questioned the wise men about their gods and their history; they sat in awe° on the banks of newly discovered rivers. Then they went back home, reflecting upon what they had seen, and perhaps they wrote a book or two about their discoveries. Slowly, nations learned about each other, men met and ideas spread—for better or worse*.

means . . . ways to travel

learned men

in . . . with fearful admiration

There was a time*, closer to ours, when artists and writers journeyed all over Europe and sometimes farther to study ancient works of art and to exchange ideas and methods with their foreign colleagues°. Poor adventurers trudged° on foot while rich travelers rode in comfort. Two centuries ago, it became fashionable for wealthy families to send their grown children to foreign countries where they would complete their education. A young man was expected to acquire good manners and a taste for° literature in France, an appreciation of music in Germany, and some feeling of history in the Roman Forum[1].

people of the same profession
walked with difficulty

taste . . . liking for

Thus all kinds of travelers learned and dreamed through the centuries. But their number was always limited, for they were only a privileged minority—the rich, the free, the talented, and the adventurous—who could enjoy a pleasure unknown by the great masses.

This is not true any more. Railroads, ships, buses, and airplanes have made travel easier, faster, and cheaper; and the number of people who can spare the time and the money to take trips has grown enormously. It is not reserved to a lucky few, nowadays, to admire Inca[2] temples, giant Buddhas, French castles, and Australian kangaroos°. Millions of people do each year. But instead of being called travelers, they are known as *tourists* and they are seen all over the world—floating down the Amazon, cruising° to Alaska, flying from Timbuktu to Easter Island, and taking pictures of Norwegian churches and Pakistani costumes.

taking a pleasure trip by boat

Surely this represents great progress. It is just and good that most of the people who dream of seeing the Parthenon should have a chance

---

[1] The Roman Forum was a meeting place in ancient Rome. The Amazon River flows through South America. Timbuktu is a very old city in Africa. Easter Island is located in the Pacific Ocean, west of Peru. The Parthenon was the temple of the goddess Athena in Athens, Greece. Machu Picchu is a ruined city high in the mountains of Peru.

[2] *Inca* is the name of the ancient kings of Peru, now applied to all Peruvians of their time.

very distant

unwanted things left on the ground / marks written on walls

at . . . slowly

students of ruins

reminder

things that make life easier annoying things

as a duty

wear . . . disappear gradually

to do so. It is satisfying to know that remote° ruins are not forgotten in deep forests, to be seen only by a few explorers at the risk of their lives*. It is excellent that people of different countries should meet and talk to each other.

But is it really?

Is it really desirable to have the most remote beach, the most hidden temple exposed to human curiosity and at the same time to the litter° and graffiti° that humanity leaves in its path? Would it be better to leave such treasures to the local population, which perhaps doesn't pay any attention to them*?

Is it better to have a few knowing admirers study a painting at leisure°, or a crowd see it in haste and confusion? The man who discovered the old Inca city of Machu Picchu in 1911 had faced extraordinary difficulties to reach it. But although dangerous and exhausting, the climb was very rewarding to him, and to the few archaeologists° who followed him later. Once in the ruined streets of the town, they could wander around, alone with the memory of the Indians who had built it centuries earlier; and perhaps they were able to make some discovery that would bring more light to a mysterious past. Today Machu Picchu is a great tourist attraction. The visitors, brought by planes, trains, and buses, walk through the city in groups. Cameras click; guides shout their explanations in several languages; people push, run up and down the steps, drop bits of litter, and perhaps take a small stone as a souvenir°. Some disappointed visitor may complain, once in a while, that this is not the most satisfying way to see a place so full of history and sadness. And of course he is right; but without the modern conveniences°—and inconveniences°—would he be able to visit Machu Picchu at all?

Finally, if you are in a bad mood, you may wonder what good, what understanding could come from the meeting of an exhausted tourist with the merchants of a city that he is visiting in three days, running dutifully° through five churches, four museums, and a row of souvenir shops.

The saddest aspect of mass tourism has been brought recently to the attention of* the public: it seems that the great number of visitors is destroying the treasures that they enjoy most. Under millions of feet, ancient stones wear out°, ancient floors break down. Parts of the palace of Versailles may have to be closed to the public in order to preserve them, and some European caves, famous for their thirty-thousand-year-old paintings, have already been closed because the paintings were damaged by human respiration. There may come a time when* only specialists in art, history, or archaeology will be allowed near the treasures of the past.

Perhaps we'd better hurry* to see them; perhaps we'd better take a tour soon.

IDIOMS AND EXPRESSIONS*

Idiom	Definition
for better or worse	with good and bad results
to be a time when	at a certain time
there was a time when artists and writers journeyed	*at a certain time, artists and writers used to journey*
there may come a time when only specialists will be allowed	*at some time in the future, only specialists may be allowed*
at the risk of their lives	with the possibility of losing their lives
to pay attention to	to be interested in, to notice
the local population doesn't pay attention to them	*the local population is not interested in them*
pay attention to what I am saying	*listen carefully to what I am saying*
to bring to the attention of	to show to
we'd better hurry	we should hurry; it would be better if we hurried

THE VOCABULARY OF TRAVEL

A tourist is a traveler who takes planned trips, called tours.

A tour usually includes many places or countries; it is often organized by a travel agent who buys all the tickets and reserves airplane seats and hotel rooms for his clients (customers).

The word "tourist" has acquired a bad meaning because of the tourists who behave badly or loudly in the places that they are visiting.

A journey is a long trip; it can be exhausting (very tiring) to journey to distant places.

An explorer is a person who visits a little-known area and studies it carefully.

An archaeologist studies the ruins of ancient cities and tries to find out how their populations lived.

One can study archaeology in college.

Brave men venture (take the risk of going) into unknown or dangerous places.

People trudge through snow, sand, or water.

Tourists use modern means of transportation: they fly in airplanes (planes), they cruise slowly in pleasure ships and boats, they ride in cars, buses, and railroad trains.

A cruise is a leisurely (slow) trip by boat with many stops in interesting places.

Tourists visit castles, palaces, and temples, and also museums, where works of art are shown to the public.

They listen to guides, who are the people paid to show places and give explanations of them.

The visitors take pictures with their cameras.

Sometimes they buy souvenirs (objects that will remind them of their trip later).

People drop litter on the ground: empty cigarette packs, bits of paper, empty bottles, etc.

They also leave graffiti (words, drawings) on the walls or on the trees.

When people are lost, or when they are not in a hurry, they wander around (walk in all directions).

A convenience is anything that makes life easier: for a modern traveler, the modern conveniences are good means of transportation, the help of a travel agent, comfortable hotels, the possibility of paying by check, and the telephone, for example.

The inconveniences, the annoying and bothering things that make life less pleasant, are the crowds, the noise, the heat, the souvenir shops, and so on.

EXERCISES

True or False?

When the statement is completely true, or completely false, answer *yes* or *no*. If the statement is only partly true, explain why in a few words.

Example: Traveling and tourism are modern activities.
   Tourism is a modern activity, but traveling is not.

1. The idea of sending students abroad is not new.

2. Traveling was so hard in ancient times that people traveled only to make money.

3. Only the rich could travel in ancient times.

4. A tourist is a traveler who takes only short trips.

5. Visitors damage old buildings and ruins in many ways.

6. Like ancient travelers, modern explorers and archaeologists need to be strong and rather brave.

7. Because of the modern conveniences, it is much more satisfying today to visit famous places.

8. It is very fortunate that ideas and customs can spread from country to country.

9. There are many more travelers now because the population of the world is larger.

10. The author says that tourists make many friends while traveling.

11. The main idea of the article is: travel is much easier now than it used to be, but it is not always better.

Vocabulary

A. 1. What *means of transportation* can you name?

   2. What is the difference between an *ancient* country and a *remote* country?

   3. What does a *guide* do?

   4. What is the difference between a *scholar* and a *student?*

   5. What do you do with a *camera?*

   6. What can a *travel agent* do for you?

B. 1. When you look at a mountain *in awe:*
   a. you look in comfort
   b. you look with fear and admiration
   c. you look without interest

   2. When a sign says "Don't *litter!*" it means that you must not:
   a. leave papers and bottles on the ground
   b. drive fast
   c. eat or drink in the place

   3. When you read that a man *ventured* inside a building, you get the feeling that:
   a. the man was walking fast
   b. the man was forced to enter the building
   c. the man took a risk by going inside the building

   4. *Graffiti* are:
   a. the remains of ancient cities
   b. objects that people take or buy as a reminder of their trip
   c. what people write or draw on walls and other places

   5. When you visit a place *at leisure,* or *leisurely,* you visit it:
   a. without spending much money
   b. alone
   c. without hurry

   6. When you *bring* a fact *to a person's attention:*
   a. you make that person notice the fact
   b. you learn the fact from that person
   c. you bring it to the person's office

C. Explain the difference in meaning between the following pairs of sentences.

   1. They are *flying* to the islands./They are *cruising* to the islands.

   2. She visited the museum *recently.*/She visited the museum *dutifully.*

   3. He *wandered* through the city./He *explored* the city.

   4. The child *trudges* to school in the snow./The child *walks* to school in the snow.

Word Forms

Complete each of the following sentences with the correct word; be sure to make the necessary changes in the nouns (singular or plural) and in the verbs (tenses). The word forms are always given in the same order: noun(s), verb, adjective(s), adverb(s).

1. *travel, traveling, traveler, to travel*

   a. Some people don't like to _____ at all.
   b. But they have to do much _____ for business anyway.
   c. Those unhappy _____ would rather stay home.
   d. Herodotus is not the only man who wrote about his _____ in ancient times.

2. *ability, to enable, able*

   a. The camel is precious in dry countries because of its _____ to survive several days without water.
   b. A horse wouldn't be _____ to do the same.
   c. The camel's sense of smell _____ this animal to locate water at a good distance.

3. *adventure, adventurer, to venture, adventurous*

   a. It took great courage to _____ alone in countries that nobody had ever visited before.
   b. Only the most _____ men would try.
   c. Some of these _____ never came back.
   d. Those who did come back had many good and bad _____ to describe.

4. *explorer, exploration, to explore*

   a. The sixteenth century has been called The Age of _____.
   b. Some brave men had _____ unknown parts of the world before.
   c. But the many _____ of the sixteenth century discovered new oceans and new continents.

5. *taste, to taste, tasty*

   a. A _____ dish is a dish that _____ good.
   b. You should _____ the soup; it is delicious.
   c. That cheese has a very strong _____.

   taste, taste for, tasteful, tastefully

   a. Herodotus had a _____ for travel.
   b. Every person has his or her own _____ in art, in clothes, in furniture.
   c. The room was furnished beautifully, _____.
   d. People do not always agree on what is _____ and what is not.

6. *convenience, convenient, conveniently/ inconvenience, to inconvenience, inconvenient*

    a. The hotel is _____ located in the center of town.
    b. We hope it is _____ for you to meet us at two o'clock.
    c. We don't want to _____you.
    d. We don't want to take that train; it arrives at a very _____ hour.
    e. All stores and museums are closed on Mondays; it's a great _____.
    f. The subway was cheap and fast; it was a great _____ .

7. *distance, distant, distantly*

    a. The ancient travelers used to cover great _____ on horseback.
    b. Peter and I belong to the same family, but we are only _____ related.
    c. He is not a friendly person; he always looks cold and _____.
    d. On their small boats, the ancient sailors sailed to very _____ lands.

8. *curiosity, curious, curiously*

    a. Cats are very _____; they always look inside boxes and explore unfamiliar rooms carefully.
    b. People say: "_____ kills the cat."
    c. We found a very strange, very _____ object in a souvenir shop.
    d. It was _____ decorated.

Synonyms

Read the following sentences aloud, replacing each italicized word with a word from the list. Give the proper form of the verbs.

privileged	nowadays	to reflect upon	in haste
to complete	specialist	remote	taste
excellent	ancient	exhausting	to be able to
to wonder	to wander		

1. Only an *expert* could tell you how old the ruins are.

2. We ate a *very good* dinner in that little restaurant.

3. *These days* you find great crowds of tourists wherever you go.

4. A few *favored* people have been allowed to visit the buildings.

5. Don't act *fast;* you might make a mistake.

6. Peter has no *liking* for archaeology.

7. *Very old* buildings don't interest him at all.

8. They had time *to think about* their adventure.

9. It was a *very tiring* journey.

10. She *could not* answer the merchants in their own language.

11. I have almost *finished* the work I started last month.

12. The ruins are in a *very distant* part of the forest.

13. He *walked around* for a long time trying to find them.

14. We were *asking ourselves* if they were really there.

Prepositions

Read aloud the following story, supplying the missing prepositions.

about   at   for   from   in   into   of   on   to

AN ANCIENT TRAVELER

We know that men have been traveling _____ thousands of years. _____ the fifth century before Christ, the Greek Herodotus became famous _____ his travels and his writings. We don't know much _____ Herodotus. We only know that he was born _____ the city of Halicarnassus, _____ the coast of modern Turkey. He began to travel when he was a young man; but he probably didn't travel _____ pleasure at first, since he was forced to leave his town _____ political reasons. A modern tourist wouldn't think that Herodotus traveled _____ comfort; but he did travel _____ leisure, going far and seeing many things. He found out that he had a taste _____ foreign countries. He went _____ Egypt, sat _____ awe _____ the bank _____ the Nile and questioned the Egyptians _____ the Pyramids, which were already very old. He learned much _____ the Egyptian priests. He also ventured _____ Persia and _____ the unknown region that is now the southern part of Russia. He asked questions _____ the places that he couldn't visit himself and received information _____ travelers who had visited them. Finally he went to live _____ Italy and wrote books _____ his experiences. The ancient world learned a great deal _____ him _____ the distant lands that they had not known before.

Idioms

A. Answer the following questions, using the idiom as shown in the example.

  Example: Don't you think you should leave now?
             Yes, I'd better leave.

  1. Don't you think you should call the guide?

  2. Don't you think we should ask the price?

  3. Don't you think I should look at the map?

  4. Don't you think he should go back to the hotel?

  5. Don't you think they should repair the floor?

  6. Don't you think we should find the bus stop?

  7. Don't you think you should take a coat?

  8. Don't you think she should pay attention to what they say?

B. Compare the tenses in the following two sentences.

  I *waited* for the train for two hours (I am not waiting any more).
  I *have been waiting* for the train for two hours (I am still waiting).

  Change the following statements to indicate that the action is not over, as shown in the example.

  Example: He organized tours.   (many years)
           He has been organizing tours for many years.

  1. I dreamed of going to Hawaii.   (a long time)

  2. They repaired the street.   (several weeks)

  3. These people took pictures of the cows.   (two hours)

  4. People admired the Parthenon.   (a very long time)

  5. He explored the banks of the Amazon.   (ten years)

  6. The local population stole stones from the ruins.   (centuries)

  7. People left graffiti on buildings.   (hundreds of years)

  8. We cruised from island to island.   (two weeks)

  9. She worked as a tour guide.   (two months)

  10. I studied English.   (_____ years)

Comparatives

Read the following sentences aloud, supplying the comparative of the adjective in parentheses. Pay attention to the meaning of the sentence, for it could be *more or less: cleaner* or *less clean, more intelligent* or *less intelligent,* for example.

1. Some travel agents have _____ (interesting) jobs than others.

2. They travel often to find out which means of transportation are _____ (fast), _____ (cheap), _____ (convenient), or _____ (elegant) than others.

3. They visit many cities and try to find out which hotels have _____ (low) prices than others, or where the rooms are _____ (beautiful) and _____ (clean) than anywhere else.

4. Some travelers do not have much money and want _____ (expensive) rooms than _____ (wealthy) tourists.

5. The agents want to know which location is _____ (far) from the station or from the museums, and which one is _____ (close) to the shopping center.

6. They choose the one that is _____ (difficult) to reach than the others.

7. They want to know whether the ride by train takes _____ (long) than the bus ride, and whether the planes of one company arrive _____ (early) or seem _____ (comfortable) than the planes of other airlines.

8. If the plane is comfortable, the trip is certainly _____ (exhausting).

9. The agents seek to know which restaurant is _____ (good), _____ (bad), or _____ (costly) than the others.

10. They see _____ (many) countries than their customers; although they are _____ (wealthy) than their clients, their trips are often _____ (satisfying), because the personnel of every hotel is _____ (eager) to please them.

Superlatives

Give a likely answer to each of the following questions, using the superlative of the italicized adjective.

Example: Is riding a camel a *comfortable* way to travel?
　　　　　Yes, it's the most comfortable way to travel.
　　　　　The most comfortable way to travel is by car.
　　　　　It's the least comfortable way to travel.
　　　　　I don't know if it's the most comfortable way.

1. Winter is a *bad* season to visit Alaska, isn't it?

2. History books are *exciting* books to read, aren't they?

3. Is climbing mountains a *dangerous* sport?

4. Is flying a *pleasant* way to travel?

5. Are *talented* artists always wealthy?

6. The *good* time to travel is October, isn't it?

7. The Andes are *high* mountains in South America, aren't they?

8. Is the South Pole an *attractive* place for a vacation?

9. Is cruising the *fast* way to go from Africa to South America?

Topics for Discussion or Composition

1. Have you seen any tourists? What were they doing? What did you note particularly?

2. Why do people travel nowadays: to learn something about other countries, to get away from their normal life, to impress their friends, to have fun, to meet people? Can you name any other reasons?

3. Do you think that the last sentence of the text is very reasonable? Why?

4. Would you like to be a travel agent?

5. Now that so many people travel, do you think that they understand other countries better?

6. Do you think that the meeting of people of different nations that way is good, bad, or makes no difference?

7. Which do you think is best: to travel in the modern way, comfortably, but with crowds of people, guides, and souvenir shops, or as the ancient travelers did— alone and in peace, but slowly and uncomfortably?

8. When ancient treasures like the Parthenon are in danger of being damaged by their visitors, what should be done: is it best to keep the place open to all visitors until the building is destroyed completely? To admit only scholars who study and appreciate it? To allow small groups in to see it once in a while (students or tourists)? To close the place to everyone to preserve it? Do you have a better idea?

9. Ideas and customs spread from country to country. Is this good or bad? Why? Can you give an example?

10. If you could travel right now, where would you go? What do you want to see or do?

For Composition Only

1. Write an outline of the main points and supporting details in this essay.

2. Have you ever taken a trip? Describe your trip briefly, explaining when you took it, where you were going, and telling what you remember most.

2

What do parents owe their children?

F I HAD to select a word that best describes the majority of American parents, that word would be *guilt-ridden*°. How sad it is to see parents become the willing victims of the "give-me game," only to discover that, no matter* what they do, it isn't enough. In the end, they are despised for their lack of firmness and blamed when their spoiled° children get into trouble*. With this in mind, I shall first answer the question: "What do parents owe their children?" and I shall start with what they don't owe them.

filled with guilt feelings

brought up without discipline

Parents don't owe their children every minute of their day and every ounce of their energy. They don't owe them round-the-clock* car service, singing lessons, tennis lessons, expensive bicycles, a motorcycle or a car when they reach sixteen, or a trip to Europe when they graduate°.

finish their school studies

I take the firm position that parents do not owe their children a college education. If they can afford it, fine; they can certainly send them to the best universities. But they must not feel guilty if they can't. If the children really want to go, they'll find a way. There are plenty of loans and scholarships° for the bright and eager who can't afford to pay.

financial help for study

After children marry, their parents do not owe them a down payment* on a house or money for the furniture. They do not have an obligation to baby-sit° or to take their grandchildren in their home when the parents are on vacation. If they want to do it, it must be considered a favor, not an obligation.

stay with a child

In my opinion, parents do not owe their children an inheritance°, no matter how much money they have. One of the surest ways to produce a loafer° is to let children know that their future is assured.

possessions left by dead parents

lazy person

Do parents owe their children anything? Yes, they owe them a great deal.

One of their chief obligations is to give their children a sense of personal worth, for self-esteem° is the basis of a good mental health. A youngster who is constantly made to feel stupid and unworthy, constantly compared to brighter brothers, sisters, or cousins, will become so unsure, so afraid of failing, that he (or she) won't try at all. Of course, they should be corrected when they do wrong; this is the way children learn. But the criticisms should be balanced with praises, preferably with a smile and a kiss. No child is ever too old to be hugged°.

respect of self

held in someone's arms

Parents owe their children firm guidance and consistent° discipline. It is frightening for a youngster to feel that he is in charge* of himself; it's like being in a car without brakes°. The parent who says "No" when other parents say "Yes" sends a double message. He is also saying: "I love you, and I am ready to risk your anger, because I don't want you to get into trouble."

unchanging

used to slow down car

Ann Landers, "What Do Parents Owe Their Children?" *Family Circle*, Nov. 1977. Used by permission of Field Newspaper Syndicate.

16

worship of person or god
religious

wrong information

right to have secrets

private notebooks

beliefs

Parents owe their children some religious training. The fact that so many strange cults° are enjoying such success is proof that children feel the need for something spiritual° in their life.

Parents owe their children a comfortable feeling about their body, and enough information about sex to balance the misinformation° that they will surely receive from their friends.

Parents owe their children privacy° and respect for their personal belongings. This means not borrowing things without permission, not reading diaries° and mail, not looking through purses, pockets, and drawers. If a mother feels that she must read her daughter's diary to know what is going on*, the communication between them must be pretty bad.

Parents owe their children a set of solid values° around which to build their lives. This means teaching them to respect the rights and opinions of others; it means being respectful to elders, to teachers, and to the law. The best way to teach such values is by example. A child who is lied to will lie. A child who sees his parents steal tools from the factory or towels from a hotel will think that it is all right to steal. A youngster who sees no laughter and no love in the home will have a difficult time laughing and loving.

No child asks to be born. If you bring a life into the world, you owe the child something. And if you give him his due*, he'll have something of value to pass along to your grandchildren.

ANN LANDERS[1]

[1] Ann Landers receives thousands of letters from people who want to tell her their problems and ask her for advice. Newspapers in the United States and many other countries publish some of these letters with Ann's answer. She has millions of readers.

IDIOMS AND EXPRESSIONS*

Idiom	Definition
no matter	it is not important
no matter what they do	*it is not important what they do; despite anything they may do*
to get into trouble	to do something that will cause difficulties or punishment from parents or police
when their spoiled children get into trouble	*when their spoiled children do something bad that will cause difficulties*
round-the-clock	at all hours of the day or night

down payment

the first partial payment on an expensive item; the rest of the price is covered in monthly installments

to be in charge

to be responsible, to control

to feel that he is in charge of himself

to feel that he alone is responsible for what he is doing

who is in charge here?

who is in control here, who is responsible?

what is going on

what is happening, what is being done

to have a difficult time doing something

to do something with difficulty

he will have a difficult time laughing and loving

it will be difficult for him to laugh and love

his due

what is owed to him

if you give him his due

if you give him what is owed to him

THE VOCABULARY OF FAMILY LIFE

Youngsters (young people) between the ages of thirteen and nineteen are sometimes called teen-agers.

Parents spoil their children by giving them too many presents and not enough discipline.

A mother hugs a child when she holds him tightly in her arms.

Parents guide their children by showing them what is right and wrong. Children need guidance; they need to learn the values (customs and beliefs) that rule people's behavior.

All the people older than you are your elders.

When parents die, their children inherit all their possessions; each child receives his or her share of the inheritance.

A baby sitter stays with a child while the parents are out. Teen-agers often baby-sit to earn some money. They play with the child, feed him, put him to bed.

A student who cannot afford college can borrow money to finance his studies; he gets a loan, which he will have to repay later.

A student who gets a scholarship (a sum of money given by the school or by some organization) will not have to repay it.

A loafer is a person who loafs—doesn't do anything, doesn't work.

The right to privacy is the right to be alone and to have one's own secrets.

A diary is a private (personal) notebook in which one writes one's thoughts, experiences, and secrets.

People communicate with each other when they are exchanging information and ideas. They can communicate by talking or writing.

Parents can help their children by giving them the right information; otherwise they will get misinformation from friends who don't know the truth.

Above all, parents should be consistent about the rules that they establish; they should not change them constantly.

The material world is the world of objects, goods, possessions; the spiritual world is the world of beliefs, religions.

EXERCISES

True or False?

When the statement is completely true or completely false, answer *yes* or *no*. If the statement is only partly true, explain why in a few words.

Ann Landers says:

1. Parents of intelligent children have a duty to send them to college.

2. A man works with more energy and confidence when he knows that he will inherit his parents' money.

3. Parents can show love by refusing something to their children, or forbidding them to do something.

4. One should never hug older children because it makes them uncomfortable.

5. Children learn much by seeing what their parents do.

6. Children prefer to be in charge of their own lives at an early age.

7. Grandparents don't have a duty to baby-sit with their grandchildren.

8. There is no way for a student without money to go to college.

9. Children shouldn't be corrected because it destroys their self-esteem.

10. It's good to compare a youngster to his brighter brothers because he tries harder.

11. What parents owe their children is not bought with money.

12. Children despise parents who are too severe.

Vocabulary

A. 1. How would you describe the "*give-me game*" between parents and children?

2. A friend of yours is working on a project. He tells you that the project has been *problem-ridden* from the beginning. What do you understand?

3. If parents are *consistent* in the way they discipline their children, does that mean that they change the rules often?

4. Someone tells you that you are a *loafer*. Are you pleased? Why?

5. What would you rather get, a *loan* or a *scholarship*? Why?

6. What do *baby sitters* do?

7. Suppose someone walks into this room and asks, "*What is going on here?*" What do you answer?

8. Paul and George are friends. Paul lends twenty dollars to George in order to help him. Later, George gives the twenty dollars back to Paul. Which friend did a *favor* to the other, and which one satisfied an *obligation*?

B. **1.** You use *brakes* in your car:
   a. to make the car go faster
   b. to make the car go backwards
   c. to make the car slow down

2. A student *graduates*:
   a. at the end of his studies
   b. when he enters college
   c. every time he gets a good grade

3. When you give a *down payment* to a car dealer:
   a. you pay in cash part of the price of a car
   b. you ask the dealer to lower the price
   c. you ask for your money back

4. The children's *spiritual needs* concern:
   a. their health
   b. their religious beliefs
   c. their education

5. When you have a *diary*:
   a. you drink it
   b. you write in it
   c. you pay your college expenses with it

Word Forms

Complete each of the following sentences with the correct word; be sure to make the necessary changes in the noun and verb forms.

1. *firmness, firm, firmly*

   a. Do you think that Ann Landers was _____ with her own daughter?
   b. The baby sitter told the little girl _____ that it was time to go to bed.
   c. The child was surprised; she was not used to such _____ .

2. *criticism, to criticize, critical, critically*

   a. Some people cannot accept _____ even from their friends.
   b. But *they* are very _____ of other people.

c. Perhaps they should look at themselves more _____ .

d. They would not get so angry when a friend _____ them.

3. *guidance, to guide, guiding*

a. It's much easier to grow up with the help of a _____ hand.

b. They don't know what to do; they need a great deal of _____ .

c. When they were young they learned moral values that _____ them all their life.

d. We'll meet you at the station and we'll _____ you to your hotel.

4. *consistency, consistent, consistently*

a. Ann Landers has always been very _____ in the advice she has given to her readers.

b. It is not always easy to act with complete _____ .

c. In all her articles, Ann Landers has maintained _____ that children have a right to privacy.

5. *information, to inform, informative*

a. Yesterday Paula _____ her parents that she was a member of a cult.

b. Her parents had read an _____ article about the cult.

c. But Paula said that the _____ was not correct.

6. *privacy, private, privately*

a. It is difficult to find some _____ in a large family.

b. I'd like to talk to you _____ for a moment.

c. The newspapers are full of details on the _____ life of famous people.

Self/Selves

Read the following sentences aloud, supplying the proper pronoun (*myself, yourself, ourselves*, etc.)

1. If I were very sure of _____ , people would say that I have a lot of *self-confidence*.

2. Paula is a *self-educated* person; she didn't go to school, but she taught _____ many things by reading and listening.

3. If you think only of _____ , you are *selfish*.

4. But those who consider other people's needs before thinking of _____ are *selfless*.

5. A *self-made* man did not inherit his fortune; he built it _____ .

6. In a *self-service* restaurant, we are supposed to help _____ and to carry our food to a table.

7. If one hurts another person while protecting _____ , it is a case of *self-defense*.

Articles

Read aloud the following story, supplying the proper article (*a, an, the*) if an article is needed.

Ann Landers says that _____ parents shouldn't play the "give-me game." They shouldn't feel that they have _____ obligation, or _____ duty to give their children all _____ things they want. They don't have to give them _____ singing lessons, _____ expensive bicycle when _____ child is in _____ high school, _____ motorcycle or _____ car when he graduates.

_____ parents who are not rich must not feel guilty if they cannot afford _____ college education. If _____ children want to go, they can get _____ loan or _____ scholarship from _____ organization. _____ parents don't have to leave their fortune to their children; telling _____ child that he will inherit is _____ best way to produce _____ loafer. _____ best gift that _____ parents can give _____ son or _____ daughter is _____ sense of _____ personal worth. This means that _____ child must not be told that he is not as good as _____ other children in _____ family. When _____ child is criticized or corrected, _____ criticism must be balanced with _____ smile and _____ affectionate hug.

Ann Landers thinks that _____ children should learn to respect _____ rights and _____ opinions of others, to be respectful to elders, to _____ teachers and to _____ law. But _____ best way to teach such values is by _____ example; _____ child who sees his father or his mother lie or steal will grow up with _____ belief that lying and stealing are all right.

So . . . That

Change the following sentences, using *"so. . . that"* as shown in the examples.

Examples: Paul won't try because he is very afraid of failing.
Paul is so afraid of failing that he won't try.

We can't buy the house because the down payment is so high.
The down payment is so high that we can't buy the house.

1. The baby sitter was asleep because it was very late.

2. John will surely get a scholarship because he is very bright.

3. We can not go on vacation because we are very busy right now.

4. I decided to buy a bicycle because motorcycles are very expensive.

5. He feels stupid by comparison because his brothers are very bright.

6. They stayed another week because the weather was very beautiful.

7. We never felt poor because there was much love in our house.

8. Ann Landers receives letters from foreign countries because she is very famous.

No Matter

In most cases, *"no matter . . ."* means *"it is not important . . ."* and it can be used in many ways.

Examples: *No matter who* you are, you are expected to obey the law.
No matter where you are, you should respect other people's customs.
No matter when you come, we'll be happy to see you.
No matter how the other parents act, a father should say "No" sometimes.
No matter how wealthy they are (*no matter how much* money they have), they don't have to leave their fortune to their children.

Read the follow statements aloud, supplying the proper *"no matter . . ."* expression in each one.

1. Many of Ann Landers' readers do not know her real name. But no _____ her real name is, she is famous everywhere as "Ann Landers."

2. She is not a young woman, but no _____ old she is, her admirers find her ageless.

3. They may find themselves in New York or in Alaska; no _____ they are, they will find her column (*newspaper article appearing regularly*) in the local newspaper.

4. Children, grandmothers, unmarried men, all sorts of people write to her. No _____ writes, the letter has a good chance to be answered.

5. Some write well, some can hardly spell; no _____ the person writes, Ann Landers will help if she can.

6. Some problems may seem silly; but no _____ silly the problem seems, it may be very serious to the writer.

7. Some very rich people ask Ann Landers for her advice; no _____ rich they are, they have problems too.

8. Some people tell her what they have done, expecting her to approve; but no _____ they expect, she gives her opinion about it.

9. Some people like her very much; but no _____ they like her, they can get very irritated by her answer.

10. Perhaps she will come to your town to give a lecture next week, or next year. No _____ she comes, perhaps you should go and see what she looks like, and what she has to say.

Should/Ought to

Change the following sentences using either *should* or *ought to*.

Example: Some parents are not interested in their children's activities.
          They should be more interested in their children's activities.
          They ought to be more interested in their children's activities.

1. The baby sitter is not very gentle with the children.

2. We are not very consistent with our rules.

3. She doesn't use her bicycle very often.

4. We don't know much about students' loans.

5. He is not very respectful of old people.

6. I don't find much information about singing lessons.

7. They don't have much self-esteem.

8. You don't drive very carefully.

Topics for Discussion or Composition

1. Do you agree with Ann Landers' article? Do you disagree with something she says?

2. Do you think that children prefer firm parents or parents who let them do what they want? Are teen-agers really frightened when they are "in charge of themselves"?

3. In another article, Ann Landers says that boys, like girls, should learn to clean house, cook, sew buttons, and wash their clothes. She says that it will make them independent from other people in the future. Do you like this idea?

4. Should boys and girls receive exactly the same education, including sex education?

5. Do children have the same right to privacy that adults have? Do parents have the right to read their children's letters and diaries, to look in their drawers? Do parents have the right to know at all times where their children are, with whom, and when they'll be home?

6. Should parents know all their children's friends? What should they do if they don't like their children's friends, or find them dangerous: should they say nothing? Should they talk to their children? Should they forbid them to see the friends? Can they do anything else?

7. If you have lived in different countries, compare the way children are raised in them. What countries can you compare?

8. Some parents feel that children should be treated like adults; that they should be present when adult friends are visiting, for example, and that they should take part in the conversation. Other parents feel that children shouldn't take part in adults' activities. Which idea do you like best?

9. Which is best: to be the oldest child in a family, the youngest child, or in between?

10. Do you think that children should inherit their parents' fortune? Should a wife inherit her husband's fortune?

For Composition Only

1. Write a brief summary of Ann Landers' piece.

2. Do you know a spoiled child? How old is he (or she)? Why do you say that the child is spoiled?

3

THE NEW VANDALS

MODERN MAN takes pleasure in fouling° his nest. This isn't   dirtying
news, but one wonders why there is more vandalism[1] and
spoiling of walls and monuments today than in the days of
the Vandals who took Rome in 477 A.D. and stole its treasures, but didn't damage its works of art. Compared to today's vandals,
the original ones seem very respectable.

These reflections were brought about* by a visit to the home of
a Portuguese hospital employee and his wife, who live with their two
children in the working-class district of London. The occasion was a
first-communion[2] party for ten-year-old José. His parents, the da Silvas,
have been in England ten years, and they have done very well for
themselves* despite their surroundings.

Their apartment is one of several hundred in a huge block built
and owned by the city. It is spotless°. The da Silvas have done all the   extremely clean
decorating and they have installed the heating system—a big expense
for them. They take great pride in* their home; but they are deeply
ashamed of the condition of the entrance halls, the stairs, the doors,
all covered with graffiti.

They have complained to local authorities. The answer was that
no government, no administration, no police can prevent the rising
tide* of spray paint°, the mad protest against society by members of
that society. "Take care of* your home," they were told, "but regard
the hallways as public property, like the streets."

spray paint can

Maria da Silva's husband went to work in a carpet factory at the
age of seven, but he can read and write, for he was allowed to study
in the afternoon. Maria, who can't, lives among people who use writing
to deface° their surroundings. She cannot understand such a waste of   destroy the appearance of
talent. Neither can she imagine why her stairs are used to throw trash°   unwanted things thrown
and garbage°. None of the da Silvas' Portuguese friends can under-   away
stand it either. So they live behind their locked and defaced doors, and   unwanted, spoiled food
the grandmother in each family has been brought over from Portugal
to watch the children at all times, on their way to school and back from
school. They are not allowed to play outside. As much as they can, the
families avoid contact with the neighborhood.

The communion party was beautiful, with delicious food and Portuguese wine. The principal of José's school was there, and so was Mr.
da Silva's boss, the head nurse at the hospital. There was also a local

---

[1] The Vandals were a people from northern Europe; they invaded Italy in the fifth century
A.D. and destroyed cities and buildings. The name *vandal* is now applied to those who
do meaningless damage around them; their destruction is called *vandalism*.
[2] A first communion is a ceremony of the Catholic faith.

Adapted from "Graffiti Painters Almost Make Original Vandals Look Decent" by Fernand
Auberjonois. Copyright 1980 Monterey Peninsula Herald Company. Used by permission.

book to keep
 photographs / feast

expressing regrets for
 something done

cleaning with a brush

caring

shocked

first letters of a name

people who believe in
 perfection

very surprising

insane . . . hospital for
 mentally sick people /
 people living in the
 hospital

tears with a knife

front wall of a house

photographer who had taken pictures of the church ceremony for the family album°. The celebration° had cost much work and money.

When the guests left, the host and hostess accompanied them down the stairs, apologizing° again and again for the graffiti. They explained that they had washed the steps and the floor of the hall that morning; but no amount of scrubbing° helped.

Who were the vandals? Mostly youngsters of families who were climbing slowly from working to middle class. Some parents were concerned°, but father and mother worked, and the children had too much time to spend on their own*. They were bored. Vandalizing the great buildings, tearing up fences, breaking off the branches of small trees, smashing windows was their way of showing their anger.

The spray paint leaves its mark everywhere in the big city, but nowhere so freely as in the modern apartment buildings that have replaced the rows of small individual houses. We are told that it is worse in New York City. Perhaps it is. The only thing that the da Silvas notice is that the richer one gets, the angrier. "Nobody would dare write on the walls of the farms in our village," Maria remarks.

The Vandals were greedy robbers who took things away, but they appreciated beauty. A Vandal of that time returning to Rome now, fifteen centuries after his first visit, would be horrified° at the sight of ancient treasures sprayed with paint, at initials° carved on the buttocks of statues. Why is beauty resented? One would think that slogans[3] painted on walls were the work of idealists° with a message. Why should idealists hate beauty?

In New York, when it became obvious that the painting disease couldn't be controlled, the city encouraged drawing in bright colors on the outside and the inside of subway trains. The result was startling°; it seemed that some insane asylum° had told its inmates° to have fun, and start an exhibition on wheels.

It doesn't matter too much when the target of the mad painters is a subway train. But why damage statues and paintings in museums? Who slashes° a picture or attacks the *Pietà*[4]? "There must be a better reason than "getting even" with* society. Doctors can only say that, in their opinion, it is just one more way of showing anger.

The da Silvas will never have clean halls and stairs so long as they live in a block of apartments built by the city. If they want to find a spotless white facade°, they must go back to the poor village where they were born.

FERNAND AUBERJONOIS

[3] A slogan is a word or a phrase used repeatedly by a company to make sure that the public remembers its products or by a political party trying to hold the attention of the public.

[4] The *Pietà* of Italian sculptor Michelangelo is a famous statue, kept in a Roman church. A few years ago a man attacked it with a hammer, damaging the face and hands.

IDIOMS AND EXPRESSIONS*

Idiom	Definition
to bring about	to cause
these reflections were brought about by a visit	*these reflections were caused by a visit*
to do well for themselves	to be successful in their affairs
they have done very well for themselves	*they have been successful*
to take pride in	to be proud of
they take great pride in their home	*they are very proud of their home*
the rising tide	the increasing amount
to take care of	to keep in good condition
on their own	alone, without control
the children had too much time to spend on their own	*the children are left alone too often*
to get even with	to take revenge on

THE VOCABULARY OF VANDALISM AND BUILDINGS

Some districts of a city have individual, one-family houses; others have only stores and office buildings.

In large cities, many families live in the same apartment building.

Some big buildings cover a whole block, from one street to the next.

The facade of the buildings is often white or gray.

The da Silvas' home is not a house but an apartment.

To reach it, they walk through the entrance hall, or hallway, up the stairs; the steps are covered with trash and garbage although there are garbage cans to throw them in.

The da Silvas come from a village, where they used to live on a farm, with a fence around the garden.

The da Silvas, afraid, lock their door with a key and a lock.

They take good care of their home: they clean and scrub it, repair it, and decorate it.

Their heating system may be a central system that heats the whole apartment; or perhaps it is a stove in each room.

The vandals in the neighborhood leave graffiti on the walls and write slogans with spray paint on the facade of the buildings and monuments.

They write their initials, or carve (cut) them in the wood with knives.

They foul their surroundings and deface the buildings.

An asylum is a hospital for the insane, or mentally ill. The inmates are the people who are kept in the asylum (or in a jail).

A celebration is a special feast to celebrate a special event or a person. The da Silvas, who organized the celebration for José in their home, were the host and the hostess; the people they had invited were the guests.

In society, people who have the same rank, the same amount of wealth, or the same kind of education are said to belong to the same class.

The working class includes the people who work with their hands, either in factories, in the fields, or in shops.

The upper class includes the very wealthy and very distinguished members of society.

The large middle class includes all people who do not belong to the working or the upper class. Wealth, education, and occupation can vary greatly among members of the middle class; they can be office workers, businessmen, or doctors.

EXERCISES

True or False?

When the statement is completely true or completely false, answer *yes* or *no*. If the statement is only partly true, explain why in a few words.

1. Today's vandals are worse than the original ones.

2. The da Silvas were rich people who spent a lot of money on their home.

3. The da Silvas were ashamed of the trash left in the hall by their Portuguese neighbors.

4. The local authorities refused to help.

5. The Portuguese families were frightened.

6. The damage was done by the poorest teen-agers in the neighborhood.

7. Teen-agers used to do the same in the da Silvas' village.

8. Vandals deface buildings and monuments in many countries.

9. The city of New York tried to use the vandals' drawings.

10. The results were quite good.

11. The only thing that today's vandals respect is beauty.

12. According to this article, boredom and anger are two of the reasons for vandalism.

Vocabulary

A. 1. What are your *initials* (the initials of your name)?

2. Is there a difference between a *closed* door and a *locked* door?

3. If a friend gives you an *album*, what do you do with it?

4. Do you know any *slogans*?

5. Would you like a *robber* to come to your house? Why?

6. If someone gets angry at you and says that you should be in an *asylum*, what does he mean?

7. What do you need to *scrub* your hands?

8. Can you compare a *facade* with a *face*?

B. 1. When you want to *express regret* for something you have done:
   a. you complain
   b. you apologize
   c. you resent
   d. you deface

2. A *feast* to honor a person or an important event is:
   a. a celebration
   b. an inmate
   c. a statue
   d. a Pietà

3. A person who believes in perfection is:
   a. an employee
   b. a guest
   c. a message
   d. an idealist

4. A building or a great statue built to honor a person or an event is:
   a. a hall
   b. a treasure
   c. a monument
   d. a fence

5. When Mrs. da Silva invites friends to her house, she is:
   a. the host
   b. the hostess
   c. the guest
   d. the boss

Synonyms

Read the following sentences aloud, replacing each of the italicized words with a word or expression from the list. Give the proper form of the nouns and verbs.

fence	to smash	to deface	to bring about
on . . . own	vandalism	to get even with	garbage
rising tide	concerned	graffiti	to regard as
to slash	horrified	to vandalize	

1. There is a great deal of school *destruction* in the cities of the world.

2. American newspaper readers were *shocked* to learn recently that the repairs in the U.S. alone were costing over six hundred million dollars a year.

3. The vandals are often youngsters who have done poorly in school and want *to take revenge on* the administration and the teachers of the school.

4. They *consider* them responsible for their failure.

5. They *spoil the appearance* of the walls and *break* the windows.

6. They *damage* the library and *cut* the covers of the books.

7. They leave *spoiled food* and *marks* everywhere.

8. Sometimes such attacks *cause* a reaction from the other students.

9. The students *caring* about the condition of their school help control it.

10. Some school principals have built a *wall* around the school.

11. But it is very difficult to control the *increase* of vandalism.

Idioms

Change the following sentences to express the same idea while using the proper idiom.

to regard as   to do well for . . . self   to get even with   on . . . own

1. The Vandals were not *considered* very nice people in their time.

2. They were not kind; they *took revenge on* everyone who tried to resist or fight them.

3. They *were successful in their affairs* for a time.

4. But when their great leader died and they were left *in charge of themselves*, they began to lose their conquests.

5. Paul can never do anything *alone.*

6. He *is never successful in his affairs.*

7. But he *considers* his fellow workers responsible for his failures.

8. And he always *takes revenge on* them for their imaginary bad deeds.

9. If Maria da Silva were *in charge of herself,* she would surely find work.

10. She would surely *be successful in her affairs.*

11. She is *considered* a very intelligent woman.

12. She is also very kind; she would not *take revenge on* the young vandals of her neighborhood.

Prepositions

Read the following sentences aloud, supplying the missing prepositions.

as   at   by   for   from   in   of   on   to   with

1. Young José has a good friend _____ school; his name is Jorge.

2. José likes to bring his friend home _____ him _____ the afternoon.

3. Compared _____ José's parents, the friend's family is wealthy.

4. Jorge's father has done well _____ himself.

5. Jorge's family lives _____ a small house surrounded _____ a fence.

6. When José brings his friend home, he apologizes _____ the trash in the hallway.

7. He is ashamed _____ the graffiti on the walls.

8. Even the door _____ the apartment has been sprayed _____ black paint.

9. José explains that his parents have complained _____ the authorities.

10. But the police can't watch all the youngsters who seem to be _____ their own _____ the neighborhood.

11. José's friend doesn't pay attention _____ the graffiti; he doesn't regard them _____ a great shame for the da Silvas.

12. He knows that José's mother takes good care _____ the apartment.

13. Besides, she takes pride _____ baking delicious cakes.

14. And Jorge takes pleasure _____ eating them.

Word Forms

Complete each of the following sentences with the correct word; be sure to make the necessary changes in the noun and verb forms.

1. *pleasure, to please, pleasant, pleasantly*

   a. The school principal found the party very _____ .
   b. He said it was a great _____ to meet Mrs. da Silva.
   c. His presence _____ the da Silvas very much.
   d. They were _____ surprised to find that he understood Portuguese.

2. *news, newspaperman, newspaper/ to renew, new, newly*

   a. Did you hear the _____ ?
   b. The da Silvas have bought a _____ carpet.
   c. Their apartment has been _____ painted.
   d. Mr. da Silva knows an American _____ who writes for the *New York Times*.
   e. The *Times* is an excellent _____ .
   f. Mr. da Silva is worried; he forgot to _____ his passport.

3. *pride, proud, proudly*

   a. José was given a watch; he is very _____ of it.
   b. He shows it _____ to all the guests.
   c. Maria da Silva looks at her son with love and _____ .

4. *celebration, celebrity, to celebrate, celebrated*

   a. There was a great _____ at the end of the war.
   b. We still _____ the day of the armistice (agreement to stop the fighting).
   c. A _____ is a famous person, a _____ painter perhaps, or an actress.

5. *apology, to apologize, apologetic, apologetically*

   a. Mr. da Silva arrives late at the hospital; he _____ to his boss.
   b. He says _____ that he did not hear the alarm clock.
   c. The head nurse accepts his _____ because he is seldom late.
   d. And he is very _____ when he is late.

6. *anger, to anger, angry, angrily*

   a. Jorge doesn't get _____ very easily.
   b. When he does, he hides his _____ anyway.
   c. But once José really _____ him.
   d. And Jorge _____ refused to play with his friend.

7. *ideal, idealist, idealism, ideal, ideally*

   a. A person who seeks perfection in art, in politics, or in anything else is an

             _____ .

   b. The sun was shining; it was the _____ day for a party.

   c. He will be disappointed because he has very high _____ .

   d. Miguel's farm was _____ located in a beautiful valley.

   e. Is it true that people lose their _____ when they get older?

Indirect Questions

Make up the indirect question (either with *I wonder . . .* or *I'd like to know . . .*) that could bring each of the following answers. Your question could begin, *I wonder who, whom, what, where, when, how, how many, how much, why.*

Examples: A <u>madman</u> tried to damage the statue.
            I wonder <u>who</u> tried to damage the statue.

            He damaged it <u>with a hammer</u>.
            I'd like to know <u>how (with what)</u> he damaged it.

            He attacked it <u>because he hated statues</u>.
            I wonder <u>why</u> he attacked it.

  1. The da Silvas left Portugal *ten years ago.*

  2. *The da Silvas* left Portugal ten years ago.

  3. They found their apartment *by looking at newspaper ads.*

  4. They pay *very little* for this apartment.

  5. They have *two children.*

  6. Mr. da Silva works *in a hospital.*

  7. His boss is *the head nurse.*

  8. The da Silvas invited *all their friends* to the party.

  9. *A local photographer* took the photos.

10. He will bring the photos *in a week.*

11. He will say *that the party was beautiful.*

12. He will thank *Mrs. da Silva.*

13. He will charge *twenty dollars* for the photos.

Past and Present Perfect

Remember that the past tense *(I was)* expresses an action that happened at a precise time and is finished.

> The Vandals *took* Rome in 447 A.D.
> José's party *was* beautiful (but it's over).

The present perfect *(I have been)* expresses an action that happened *sometime* in the past, or an action that started in the past and is still going on.

> The da Silvas *have installed* a heating system (sometime in the past).
> They *have been* in England ten years (and they are still there).

Read the following sentences aloud, supplying the proper form of the verbs in parentheses. Some changes may be necessary in the placement of the adverbs.

1. Miguel and Maria da Silva _____ (to work) hard all their lives.

2. When he _____ (to be) young, Miguel _____ (to live) in Portugal.

3. His father _____ (to own) a fishing boat and _____ (to go) fishing every day.

4. The Portuguese always _____ (to be) great fishermen.

5. When Miguel _____ (to reach) the age of seven, his father _____ (to send) him to work in a factory.

6. The factory still exists; it _____ (to make) beautiful carpets for hundreds of years.

7. Miguel's son José _____ (to hear) a great deal about the factory but he never _____ (to see) it.

8. Young Miguel _____ (to work) all morning in the factory; he _____ (to earn) a very small salary.

9. In the afternoons, he _____ (to learn) how to read and write.

10. Over the years, Mr. da Silva _____ (to read) quite a few books.

11. At twenty, Miguel _____ (to marry) Maria; he then _____ (to decide) to go to England.

12. He _____ (to want) to start a new life.

13. The da Silvas _____ (to be) happy in London; but at first Maria _____ (to dislike) the city.

14. When he arrived in London, Miguel _____ (to go) to see another Portuguese, who _____ (to be) working in a hospital.

15. This man _____ (to help) him get a job.

16. Since that time, Mr. da Silva _____ (to do well) for himself.

17. He _____ (to make) many friends.

18. One day he _____ (to meet) a newspaper man who _____ (to write) Mr. da Silva's story for his newspaper.

Topics for Discussion or Composition

1. Have you seen any graffiti that were particularly ugly, particularly interesting, or particularly funny? Where were they and what were they like?

2. If you have lived in different countries, have you found that the graffiti and vandalism situation is different from country to country? What is the difference?

3. Is it true that there is less vandalism in country villages than in big cities?

4. People write graffiti for different reasons. In your opinion,
   a. Why does someone carve initials on a park bench or on a school desk?
   b. Why does someone write on the walls of a neighbor's house?
   c. Why might someone attack a painting or a statue in a museum?
   d. Why take the trouble of stealing a large quantity of paint and (with difficulty) painting something on the side of a bridge, or a mountain? Do you feel that the person who does this has the same reasons that the vandals in questions a and b have?

5. When vandals are caught, should they be punished? How?

6. What can be done to protect a school from vandalism?

7. Who vandalizes a school?

8. Do you prefer to live in an apartment building or in a house, when you live in a city? Why?

9. Why were the da Silvas and their neighbors frightened?

10. What needs to be done to keep a house in good condition, inside and outside?

For Composition Only

1. Write a short description of a celebration in your house: a birthday party, a religious celebration, a wedding, or any other happy occasion.

2. In your own words, make a short summary of what you have learned about vandalism from the article: who are the modern vandals? What do they do? Where do they do their damage? Why do they act in such a way?

message
to
the
un-
known

4

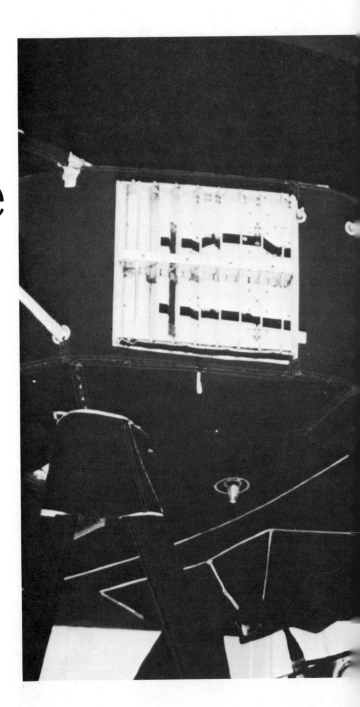

TWO SPACESHIPS named Voyager I and II were launched° in 1977 toward Jupiter, Saturn, and possibly Neptune. After collecting and sending back to us precious information about those giant planets, they will leave the solar system[1] in 1989. Nobody can tell how long their wandering will last afterwards; for distances in space are so enormous that the ships may float there for a billion years without hitting any object that could destroy them. According to the scientists, the Voyagers may get "close" to the nearest star on their path in forty thousand years or so*; in another four hundred thousand years, one of the Voyagers may pass "near" a second star. This means that in either case the ships will be at a distance of one or two light-years from the star. There won't be any crash: a light-year is the distance that light, traveling at 186,000 miles per second, can cover in 365 of our days.

sent into space

There are countless° stars in the universe. It is believed that some of them are, like our sun, circled by a number of planets; and some planets may be carrying intelligent beings, perhaps more advanced than we are°. It is therefore possible that, in a million years or so, some "creatures," flying through space in their own ships, will come upon* one of the Voyagers. The stars are so far apart that the chances of such a meeting are very small; but it is not totally impossible. The scientists who were preparing the spaceships for their journey decided to put a message on each of them. "We may never have another opportunity," they explained, "to communicate with our distant neighbors—to let someone know, some time, somewhere, that our blue planet was once the home of fairly intelligent people, more or less* civilized."

too numerous to be counted

more . . . knowing more than we do

The first difficulty was to decide what form the message should take. How can you communicate with beings that you can't even imagine? Since the laws of physics are believed to be the same throughout the universe, all beings must "see" light and "hear" sound in some way, even if they don't have eyes and ears like ours. After considering the problem carefully, the scientists and their chief, Dr. Sagan, concluded that the best way to deliver the message was to put it on a special record capable of reproducing images and sounds. It would be packed with a needle and a drawing showing how the equipment should be used.

A small committee° of scientists, writers, artists, and musicians was given the task of preparing the message itself. Despite some differences of opinion about the choice of material, the members of the committee agreed on the main points; they all said that it was essential to indicate

working group

---

[1] The solar system (system of the sun) includes our sun, which is a star, and nine planets: Mercury, Venus, Earth, Mars, the four giants Jupiter, Saturn, Uranus, and Neptune, and small Pluto. Space and all the heavenly bodies in it form the universe.

the location of Earth in the universe, to show what it looked like, and to give an idea of* the richness and variety of its cultures[2].

The message lasts two hours. It starts with 116 pictures without sound, beginning with a drawing of the solar system and photos of Earth taken from space. Life is described first with representations of a man, a woman, a mother feeding a baby, a group of older children, and a family. To show that Earthlings° live in societies, there are also pictures of people eating, working, cooking, and playing together. Then come all sorts of people: dancers, fishermen, members of different races and cultures. There are trees, beaches and islands, leaves and snow-flakes, an active volcano°, and even an earthquake. There are animals, from the bee to the elephant. Human achievements are represented by some of our most impressive buildings and bridges, along with° ordinary houses from various parts of the world. Pictures of tools and machines have been included; medical and scientific instruments; a supermarket, a busy airport, and the launching of a spaceship. And a flock of birds flying across a gorgeous° sunset.

After this silent description of our world, the record provides the earth's sounds. This section of the message begins with brief speeches in fifty-five languages (including languages that have not been used in thousands of years), plus a special greeting from a group of whales°. The speeches are followed by the sounds of nature (waves, wind, rain, animal calls, and bird songs) and human noises such as footsteps, heartbeats, the crying of a baby, men sawing wood, trucks and auto-mobiles, and—most difficult to record—the sound of a kiss.

Three quarters of the record consists of* music. This was the most difficult selection of all, for each member of the committee had his or her favorite composer°. But again they agreed finally that the aliens° should have a chance to meet as many cultures, past and present, as possible. If the finders of a Voyager can "hear" at all, they will have a wide choice: Bach, Beethoven, jazz music, a Navajo chant, folk songs from a number of countries, European music of the fifteenth century, a wedding song from Peru, melodies from Japan and India, and a very old tune from New Guinea, totally different from anything else on the record. The aliens will also hear a Mexican band, some rock-and-roll, and an ancient Chinese melody, "Flowing Streams," performed on a four thousand-year-old instrument.

The gold-covered record and its equipment, wrapped in aluminum for extra protection, are expected to survive in space for at least a billion years. What sort of beings, if any, will find them? And how will they feel about it? Will they be curious and excited? Or will they be so used to picking up* spaceships that they will be bored to find one more? Will

people on Earth

along . . . with

very beautiful

person who invents music /
strangers

[2] The culture of a people is made up of the arts, ideas, customs, and ways of life of the members of the group.

their own history and experiences help them understand what Dr. Sagan's team was trying to show? Will they be impressed by our achievements? Or will they laugh at our clumsy° efforts to communicate—if they can laugh? Will they try to locate the blue planet?   awkward, poorly done

The sad fact is—we'll never know.

The following is a list of the pictures and sounds in the Voyager message. The vocabulary does not need to be researched or memorized.

THE VOYAGER MESSAGE

Pictures (in sequence)
calibration circle
solar location map
mathematical definitions
physical unit definitions
solar system parameters
the sun
solar spectrum
Mercury
Mars
Jupiter
Earth
Egypt, Red Sea, Sinai Peninsula, Nile (from orbit)
chemical definitions
DNA structure
DNA structure magnified
cells and cell division
anatomy
human sex organs (drawing)
conception diagram
conception photo
fertilized ovum
fetus diagram
fetus
diagram of male and female
birth
nursing mother
father and daughter (Malaysia)
group of children

diagram of family ages
family portrait
continental drift diagram
structure of earth
Heron island (Australia)
seashore
Snake River, Grand Tetons
sand dunes
Monument Valley
leaf
fallen leaves
sequoia
snowflake
tree with daffodils
flying insect, flowers
vertebrate evolution diagram
seashell
dolphins
school of fish
tree toad
crocodile
eagle
South African waterhold
Jane Goodall, chimpanzees
sketch of bushmen
bushmen hunters
Guatemalan man
Balinese dancer

Andean girls
Thai craftsman
elephant
Turkish man with beard and glasses
old man with dog and flowers
mountain climber
Cathy Rigby
Olympic sprinters
schoolroom
children with globe
cotton harvest
grape picker
supermarket
diver with fish
fishing boat, nets
cooking fish
Chinese dinner
licking, eating, drinking
Great Wall of China
African house construction
Amish construction scene
African house
New England house
modern house
house interior with artist and fire
Taj Mahal
English city (Oxford)
Boston

UN building (day)
UN building (night)
Sydney Opera House
artisan with drill
factory interior
museum
X-ray of hand
woman with microscope
Pakistan street scene
India rush-hour traffic
modern highway
Golden Gate Bridge
train
airplane in flight
airport (Toronto)
Antarctic expedition
radio telescope
book page (Newton's *System of the World*)
astronaut in space
Titan Centaur launch
sunset with birds
string quartet
violin with score

Greetings in Many Tongues (alphabetically)
Akkadian
Amoy
Arabic
Aramaic
Armenian
Bengali
Burmese
Cantonese
Czech
Dutch
English

French
German
Greek
Gujarati
Hebrew
Hindi
Hittite
Hungarian
Ila
Indonesian
Italian

Japanese
Kannada
Kechua
Korean
Latin
Luganda
Mandarin
Marathi
Nepali
Nguni
Nyanja

Oriya
Persian
Polish
Portuguese
Punjabi
Rajasthani
Roumanian
Russian
Serbian
Sinhalese
Sotho

Spanish
Sumerian
Swedish
Telugu
Thai
Turkish
Ukranian
Urdu
Vietnamese
Welsh
Wu

(continued on next page)

Sounds of Earth (in sequence)

whales	cricket, frogs	laughter	riveter	auto gears
planets (audio analog of	birds	fire	Morse code	Saturn 5 rocket liftoff
orbital velocity)	hyena	tools	ships	kiss
volcanoes	elephant	dogs (domestic)	horse and cart	baby
mud pots	chimpanzee	herding sheep	horse and carriage	life signs: EEG, EKG
rain	wild dog	blacksmith shop	train whistle	pulsar
surf	footsteps and	sawing	tractor	
	heartbeats	tractor	truck	

Music (in sequence)

Bach: Brandenburg Concerto #2, 1st movement
Java: court gamelan—"Kinds of Flowers"
Senegal: percussion
Zaire: Pygmy girls' initiation song
Australia: horn and totem song
Mexico: mariachi—"El Cascabel"
Chuck Berry: "Johnny B. Goode"
New Guinea: men's house
Japan: shakuhachi (flute)—"Depicting
  the Cranes in their Nest"
Bach: Partita #3 for violin
Mozart: "Queen of the Night" (from "The Magic Flute")
Georgia (USSR): folk chorus—"Chakrulo"
Peru: pan pipes

Louis Armstrong: "Melancholy Blues"
Azerbaijan: two flutes
Stravinsky: "Rite of Spring" conclusion
Bach: Prelude and Fugue #1 in C Major
Beethoven: Symphony #5, 1st movement
Bulgaria: shepherdess song—"Izlel Delyo hajdutin"
Navajo: night chant
English 15th century: "The Fairie Round"
Melanesia: pan pipes
Peru: woman's wedding song
China: ch'in (zither)—"Flowing Streams"
India: raga—"Jaat Kahan Ho"
Blind Willie Johnson: "Dark Was the Night"
Beethoven: String Quartet #13, "Cavatina"

The Voyager Record

IDIOMS AND EXPRESSIONS*

Idiom	Definition
according to	as told by
according to the scientists	*as told by the scientists; the scientists say*
or so	about
in forty thousand years or so	*in about forty thousand years*
to come upon	to find by chance
some creatures will come upon the Voyagers	*some creatures will find the Voyagers*
more or less	partially, perhaps
more or less civilized	*partially civilized, perhaps*
to give an idea of	to show a general view of
to consist of	to be made of, to include
three quarters of the record consists of music	*three quarters of the record is music*
to pick up	to collect

THE VOCABULARY OF SPACE

The <u>universe</u> includes all of existing <u>space</u> with its countless <u>stars</u>, <u>planets</u>, and other bodies.

The <u>solar system</u> consists of the sun and the nine planets, which <u>circle</u> (go around) it and receive light from it.

The stars are so far from us and from each other that the distances cannot be calculated in miles, but in <u>light-years</u>, representing the distance <u>covered</u> (traveled) by light in one year.

Light travels at the speed of 186,000 miles <u>per second</u>.

Different types of spaceships have been <u>launched</u> (sent into space); some were carrying <u>astronauts</u> (people traveling in spaceships) and some were not.

THE VOCABULARY OF MUSIC AND SOUNDS

Through our <u>ears</u>, we <u>hear</u> <u>sounds</u>; some are pleasant.

The unpleasant ones are called <u>noises</u> rather than sounds.

The most beautiful sounds are the sounds of <u>music</u>.

The person who invents music is a <u>composer</u>.

<u>Musicians</u> play on <u>musical instruments</u> music that the composer has <u>composed</u>.

A <u>song</u> is a <u>melody</u> (or <u>tune</u>) with words.

Usually, a tune is a simple melody. A <u>chant</u> is a simple tune repeated over and over.

The Navajo night chant was sung by men from the American Indian tribe called the Navajos.

A <u>band</u> is a small group of musicians playing together.

A large group of musicians is an <u>orchestra</u>.

Some bands <u>perform</u> <u>jazz</u> music, a popular form of music first played by Negro musicians in the south of the United States.

<u>Rock-and-roll</u> music is a contemporary form of popular music.

<u>Folk music</u> consists of tunes and songs inherited from the past.

Normally, <u>records</u> only reproduce sounds, with the help of a special <u>needle</u>.

EXERCISES

Understanding the Text

1. What are the Voyagers doing in the solar system?

2. What is the solar system?

3. Will the Voyagers come back to Earth when their job is done?

4. Will they often pass near a star?

5. Do scientists think that there are more than nine planets in the universe?

6. Are scientists sure that the Voyagers will be found by aliens? Why?

7. Why did they send a record with sounds and images?

8. Did scientists prepare the message itself?

9. What did they want aliens to learn about Earth?

10. Why include *groups* of people?

11. What kind of sounds did they put on the record?

12. How did the committee show that humans were skillful and intelligent?

13. Why did they include languages that are not spoken now?

14. Did they include only human "speeches"?

15. Why did they record so many different types of music?

16. Why did the scientists try to make the record last so long in space?

Vocabulary

1. When you are *collecting* facts, you are:
   a. gathering them
   b. explaining them
   c. saying that they are not true
   d. changing them to make them right

2. A girl is *gorgeous* when she is:
   a. very intelligent
   b. very fat
   c. very sick
   d. very beautiful

3. A *clumsy* speech is:
   a. very good
   b. not well made
   c. full of information
   d. interesting

4. Someone who makes *countless* mistakes, makes:
   a. many mistakes
   b. few mistakes
   c. funny mistakes
   d. light mistakes

5. An *alien* is:
   a. a simple tune
   b. a stranger
   c. an unpleasant sound
   d. a folk musician

6. A *committee* is:
   a. a working group
   b. a group of musicians
   c. a man who writes music
   d. a group of stars

Synonyms

Read the following sentences aloud, replacing each italicized word or expression with a word or expression from the list. Be sure to make all necessary changes in nouns and verbs.

to locate	essential	to cover	giant *(adj.)*
achievement	or so	committee	to launch
to assume	to pick up	to give an idea	alien
capable of (doing)	to locate	to come upon	according to

1. The Voyagers were *sent into space*, one at a time, in August and September 1977.

2. *The scientists said that* Voyager I would reach Jupiter in March 1979, and it did.

3. It was expected to reach Saturn in November 1980, after *going* over 74,700 miles between the two *huge* planets.

4. Dr. Sagan's *working group* had *about* four weeks to prepare the message.

5. The scientists *believed without being sure* that the *strangers* would have some way to "hear" and "see."

6. They thought that anyone *able to* float through space would be very intelligent.

7. Some people said that the spaceship itself was the *most important* part of the message.

8. It *gives a general view* of human *doings*.

9. The creatures who *happen to find* a Voyager may be very interested in it.

10. Maybe they will study the strange object that they *have collected*.

11. Maybe they will try to *find* our planet, if it is still there.

12. *Time magazine says that* the two Voyagers are following different paths.

Make a few sentences of your own, starting with *according to*.

Word Forms

Complete each of the following sentences with the correct word; be sure to make the necessary changes in the noun and verb forms.

1. *collection, to collect, collective, collectively*

   a. The committee _____ melodies from all over the world for the Voyager record.
   b. They gathered a very large _____ .
   c. The message was not assembled by one person; it was a _____ effort.
   d. _____ , the songs give a good idea of the planet's cultures.

2. *circle, to circle, circular*

   a. The earth _____ the sun in 365 days.
   b. But its path is not exactly _____ .
   c. Can you draw a perfect _____ ?

3. *imagination, to imagine, imaginative*

   a. Some writers have tried to _____ how the aliens living on other planets look.
   b. Some of these writers have a great deal of _____ .
   c. If they were not _____ they couldn't write successful books, could they?

4. *safety, to save, safe, safely*

   a. When men were sent to the moon, every precaution was taken for their _____ .
   b. They did land _____ on the moon.
   c. If they had not, who could have _____ them?
   d. When they were back on Earth, everyone was happy to see them _____ .

5. *science, scientist, scientific, scientifically*

   a. The Sagan committee included writers, musicians, and a few _____ .
   b. Writers of novels about other planets often claim that their stories are
      _____ correct.
   c. They claim to have a serious knowledge of _____ .
   d. They read _____ books and magazines.

6. *location, to locate, local, locally*

   a. We heard folk music played by a _____ band.
   b. The band is not known in the rest of the country, but it is _____
      famous.
   c. Some people said that the record should not have shown the _____
      of the earth.
   d. They think that it is dangerous to help some evil aliens _____ us.

7. *difference, to differ, different, differently*

   a. The fifty-five greetings on the record are all _____ from each
      other.
   b. The _____ is in the text as well as in the language.
   c. It should have been planned _____ .
   d. The messages should not _____ in their meaning.

8. *richness, to enrich, rich, richly*

   a. Each country can display a _____ variety of music and songs.
   b. The dancers on the picture are _____ dressed.
   c. The aliens will perhaps admire the _____ of their costumes.
   d. Listening to the record will be even for the Earthlings an interesting experience
      that will _____ them.

Articles

Read aloud the following sentences, supplying the proper article *(a, an, the)* if an
article is needed.

1. _____ spaceship called Voyager is on its way to _____ three great planets,
   Jupiter, Saturn, and Neptune.

2. During _____ long journey through _____ solar system, Voyager will take
   _____ pictures of the planets.

3. Then it will begin _____ endless trip through space.

4. _____ scientists who launched Voyager use _____ computers to follow its journey.

5. According to _____ computers, Voyager will be near _____ star in forty thousand years.

6. _____ name of _____ star is AC 793888.

7. Voyager carries _____ record, _____ interesting record.

8. Usually, _____ records reproduce _____ sounds only.

9. But _____ record on Voyager can reproduce _____ pictures too, in _____ special way.

10. _____ beings who will find _____ record will be able to see _____ trees, _____ humans, and _____ animals.

11. They will see _____ elephant and _____ snowflake.

12. They will also see _____ airport and _____ launching of _____ spaceship.

13. Among _____ pictures carried by _____ record there is _____ picture of _____ man on _____ horse.

14. Some of _____ scientists say that _____ "space beings" will think it is _____ animal with four legs and two arms.

Relative Pronouns: Who, Whom, Which, Whose

Who represents a person, subject of the verb:
> The people *who* wrote the message were not all scientists.

Whom represents a person, object of the verb:
> That man, *whom* I had met before, turned out to be Dr. Sagan.
> The people *with whom* he was working were all old friends.

Which represents things, either subject or object of the verb:
> The record, *which* was covered with gold, will survive a long time in space. It has an aluminum cover, on *which* were written some instructions.

Whose is used instead of *of whom* or *of which:*
> Linda Sagan, *whose* husband is Dr. Sagan, was a member of the committee.

Replace the blanks in each of the following sentences with the proper relative pronoun.

1. Dr. Sagan, _____ was head of the committee, has written a book _____ title is *Murmurs of Earth**.

* Carl Sagan, *Murmurs of Earth* (New York: Random House, Inc., 1978).

2. The book, _____ was published in 1978, is full of information and pictures, many of _____ are in color.

3. The aliens for _____ the message was prepared may find it difficult to understand.

4. Some Earthlings _____ are not used to scientific language may find it difficult too.

5. For example, those of you _____ are curious may wonder how the position of Earth in the universe could be shown.

6. The scientists in charge of this task, _____ was difficult indeed, decided to use pulsars.

7. There are a number of objects in the universe from _____ we receive strong radio signals; we call them pulsars.

8. The length of time between two of these radio signals, _____ is called a period, is different for each pulsar.

Pulsars

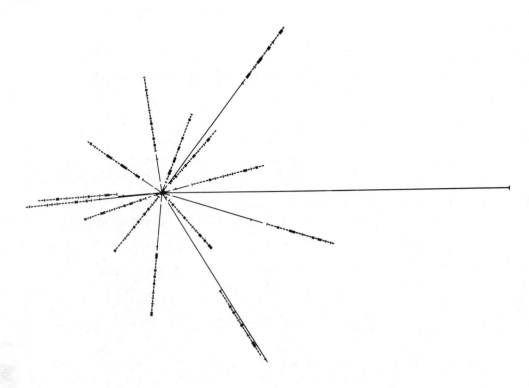

9. The aliens, to _____ pulsars will surely be known, will see on the record cover a drawing, in _____ the sun is represented by a dot.

10. Fourteen lines connect that dot to fourteen pulsars, _____ period is carefully indicated.

11. If they recognize the periods, _____ will always remain the same, the aliens will be able to locate the solar system (if it is still there).

12. Dr. Sagan, _____ you may have seen on television, is an astronomer.

13. An astronomer is a person _____ studies the universe, including the stars, planets, and pulsars.

14. Several of the people on the committee were men and women with _____ Dr. Sagan had worked before.

15. One of them is Dr. Drake, _____ Dr. Sagan surely meets often since they both teach astronomy in the same university.

16. There was also Dr. Sagan's wife, _____ is an artist, and a writer-artist named Jon Lomberg, _____ main interests are music and astronomy.

17. The members of the committee hope that the Voyager record, _____ they prepared with such care, will not be damaged in space and will be found in good condition by the aliens for _____ it was made.

Combining Sentences

A. Combine the two parts of the following sentences, using *before* + *gerund*.

Example: The Voyagers will collect information; then they'll send it to us.
The Voyagers will collect information before sending it to us.

1. The committee considered several possibilities; then they decided to make a record.

2. The committee consulted several Chinese; then they chose "Flowing Streams."

3. Dr. Sagan looked everywhere for a record of that melody from India; he found it in a restaurant.

4. The Voyager record shows pictures of Earth; then it gives the sounds of the planet.

5. The record gives fifty-five human speeches; then it adds a message from the whales.

6. They recorded many loud noises; then they tried to record a kiss.

7. The engineers tested (tried) the spaceships many times; then they launched them.

8. Our spaceships have studied the nearest planets; now they explore the distant ones.

9. Dr. Sagan completed the message; then he wrote an interesting book about it.

B. Do the same exercise again, using *after* + *gerund*.

Example: The Voyagers will collect information; then they'll send it to us.
After collecting information, the Voyagers will send it to us.

Topics for Discussion or Composition

1. Was the article interesting? Why?

2. You are friends of Dr. Sagan in 1977. He has just told you that he is thinking of putting a message on the Voyagers. Tell him what you think of his idea, and why it is good or bad.

3. The decision has been made that there will be a message on Voyager I and II. Tell Dr. Sagan what you think there should be in that message.

4. You are a member of the committee, and you object to some of the items chosen. Which ones?

5. Someone blamed the committee for showing only good or beautiful things, such as natural sights, great achievements of mankind, happy people, and peaceful situations. That person said that the message should include pictures of war, disasters, diseased people, and poverty. Do you agree with that person or do you agree with the committee?

6. Other people blamed Dr. Sagan for showing the location of Earth in the universe. They said it was very dangerous, that Earth would be attacked, invaded, destroyed. Do you agree?

7. Some people believe that our planet has already been discovered by aliens from other worlds. Some say that they came a long time ago; some say that they visit it often. What do you think? Why?

8. The Voyager record is now on sale as an ordinary record without images. Do you see any reason to sell it to Earthlings? Could it be more interesting to Earthlings than to other beings?

9. We are people living on a different planet around some star. We are back home after visiting the planet Earth and we try to describe it to our curious friends.

They want to know what Earth looks like, what the Earthlings are like, and how they behaved when they met us.

10. Would you like to go in a spaceship? Why?

For Composition Only

1. Suppose that a friend of yours doesn't know anything about the Voyagers. Write a short letter to tell your friend about the Voyager project and about the record carried by the spaceships. Give only the main facts.

2. Write a brief composition, saying whether or not you like music, what kinds of music you like and dislike, and why.

5

Helping Hands

T IS IMPOSSIBLE to find out exactly how many volunteers[1] are at work* today in the United States. Thirty-seven million or so are known to belong to organizations like the Pink Ladies, Travelers' Aid, or Big Brothers; but those who work alone or in small informal° groups cannot be counted. The total number of men and women who give their time to help others appears to be between fifty and sixty-eight million.

not organized

They do almost anything: they sew, clean, scrub, paint, cook, repair things, record books for the blind, amuse sick children in hospitals, or escort° senior citizens° who do not want to go out alone. They give their blood; they work in libraries and schools; they translate documents° for new citizens with a language problem or raise money* to support local symphony orchestras; they answer the telephone calls of the desperate who are thinking of killing themselves, and who need a friendly ear*.

go out with /
senior . . . older
people
important papers

Volunteers start community projects too small to attract the attention of organized agencies, or work at jobs for which no funds° are available. A handful° of city folk will turn an empty lot into a playground for the children of their neighborhood; others decide to repair and paint a few dilapidated° houses in their street. Somewhere else women cook and deliver two hot meals a day to elderly people living alone, and too sick or too tired to prepare their own food. Another group calls lonely old people once a day to chat a little and find out if they are all right. Some college students teach English, mathematics, or drawing to the inmates of a local jail. Young men and women spend part of their weekends collecting empty cans and bottles for the recycling center[2] of their community, and some children pick up the trash left on the beach by the crowd of a summer holiday. Anywhere one looks, the army of volunteers is hard at work*—not only in the United States, but in many other countries where "volunteerism" is spreading.

money
small number

in very bad condition

Fifteen years ago, the typical volunteer was a married woman between twenty-five and forty-five, who had children in school and time on her hands*. She was rather well educated, with a high-school or a college degree, and she didn't need to earn a salary. She was therefore free to devote her time and talents to those who seemed to

---

[1] Volunteers are people who offer to do some work without pay; here, they offer to help people in need or serve their community. The Pink Ladies (now called the "Auxiliaries" since men have joined their ranks) do all sorts of nonmedical jobs in hospitals. Travelers' Aid members are available in railroad stations and airports to help travelers who are lost, ill, in need of money, or unable to understand the language of the country. The Big Brothers are young men who volunteer to be the friend of a boy who is on his own or in trouble.

[2] In an effort to reduce the volume of trash and the use of natural resources, some industries are recycling (using again) the paper of old newspapers, the metal of used cans and the glass of empty bottles. Cans and bottles are collected and crushed at recycling centers staffed with volunteers.

need them. Some women volunteered out of* boredom, because they needed to find an occupation outside their house. But the great majority were prompted° only by the desire to relieve some distress, to be useful. There have always been such women (and men who had time to spare) ready to give of themselves* unselfishly and quietly. At the beginning of the American Civil War, around 1861, a schoolteacher named Clara Barton undertook° to deliver to wounded soldiers all sorts of supplies— clothes, food, tobacco, and even medicine—that they could not get easily. She paid for these out of* her own money at first, and later from the funds that she could collect from other generous people. She also ventured on the battlefields, during or after battles, to help the wounded and the dying. After the war, the government asked her to help search for missing soldiers. She helped later in other wars in Europe and attracted a number of women willing to share her work. The group grew and eventually became the American Red Cross, which now counts about 1,360,000 volunteers, with a budget of eighty-two million dollars, all from voluntary contributions.

Another pioneer° of the same period, Dorothea Dix, fought to improve the living conditions in the "hospitals" for the mentally ill, which were not well run at the time. Her efforts finally caused state governments to take financial responsibility for these institutions. Many organizations have been launched by a determined group of volunteers, from the Boy Scouts and Girl Scouts of America to the Sierra Club, devoted to the protection of nature, and to the Gray Panthers, who fight discrimination° against the elderly and try to keep them active, happy, and politically important by encouraging them to vote.

The early volunteers deserve special respect and admiration, for they were working alone and doing hard and unpleasant tasks. Often they were regarded by the authorities as troublemakers rather than angels. The situation improved as their number grew and as society became aware of their achievements. Gradually, the volunteers began to receive funds from private sources and from the government. They organized themselves, they became professional, and they did a considerable amount of good work. Then, in the last ten or fifteen years, changes in society brought about a transformation of volunteerism.

What changes? In the first place, the number of women, married or unmarried, who can afford to work without pay has been greatly reduced by the present economic conditions. Secondly, it has become more and more difficult for all would-be workers° without training to find employment. Those job-seekers—the young, the unskilled, and the women who must now earn a salary—have discovered that the best way to get hired is to acquire some working experience. The result has been a considerable increase in the number of volunteers in recent years, as well as a change in their reasons for serving.

There is no "typical" volunteer nowadays; volunteers come from

Margin glosses:

caused to act

took the task of

early leader

special attitude against

would-be . . . those wanting to be workers

all levels of society, all races and age groups, and their motives° are   reasons to act
varied. Charity and kindness are still playing a large role: the one
hundred thirty-five thousand men and women who have become volunteer "grandparents" for lonely youngsters, and who spend hours
with their "grandchild" in hospitals, playgrounds, jails, or homes for
the retarded and the handicapped[3], are certainly not working for selfish
reasons. But many other volunteers have been forced by circumstance
to try to help themselves while helping others. Perhaps it is a high-
school girl spending a summer in a hospital to find out what it is like*
to be a nurse before she enters nursing school. Perhaps it is a student
or an uneducated person trying to get some training in a field where
he hopes to find a paying job later. Even men and women aiming at
high positions know that their volunteer experience can help them get
what they want. For many volunteers are used to doing difficult or
important work—they raise funds on a large scale, they organize and   groups of workers /
direct large staffs°, they conduct board meetings° and deal with official   board . . . meetings of
agencies. Such training is often more interesting to an employer than   the directors
the academic° knowledge of a brand-new° graduate; and the person   learned in school /
who arrives with ten years of experience in the right kind of volunteer   perfectly new
work and the recommendation of a respected volunteer agency may
well be chosen first.

It would be a mistake to conclude that unselfish concern has disappeared. Even if they have to consider their own problems, volunteers
are still prompted by their hearts. They join because they care. They
are anxious to bring a smile to the face of the old, the young, or the
lonely person whom they are helping. "It is good to get out of your
own happy circle, and to ask yourself questions," says a French volunteer.

The number of volunteer agencies is now so large (one hundred
thirty-seven thousand in the United States alone), that special organizations had to be created to coordinate° their work. These organizations   organize together
do their best to attract volunteers, direct them toward the agency that
can use their particular skill, and in general try to help the volunteer
force work smoothly. Some volunteers feel rather unhappy about the
professional and very organized aspect of the agencies; they prefer to
help the needy, informally, in their own neighborhood. And they can
find plenty to do. One may wonder what Clara Barton and Dorothea
Dix would think of the number and efficiency° of today's volunteers,   producing good results
if they could see them. Since they were very efficient women them-   without waste
selves, they would probably be pleased.

[3] Handicapped children are suffering from serious physical problems; retarded children
are those whose minds have not developed normally.

IDIOMS AND EXPRESSIONS*

Idiom	Definition
at work	working
hard at work	working hard
to raise money	to collect money
a friendly ear	someone who listens like a friend
to turn into	to change into; to transform into
to have time on her hands	to have more than enough time
out of	because of, because, with
women volunteered out of boredom	*women volunteered because they were bored*
she paid for the supplies out of her own money	*she paid for the supplies with her own money*
to give of themselves	to give their time, work, and effort
what is it like?	how does it feel?
to find out what it is like to be a nurse	*to find out how it feels to be a nurse, whether it is pleasant or unpleasant*

THE VOCABULARY OF VOLUNTEERISM

Volunteers are people who care for others.
They want to help elderly people, or handicapped or retarded children; to relieve some distress (suffering) or to be useful in any other way.

They escort senior citizens who cannot or do not want to go out alone. The expression *senior citizens* is often used nowadays for *older people*.

They translate English documents into the language that is understood by the person who received it.

The typical (average) volunteer used to be a woman with time on her hands.

She volunteered for different reasons; but her motives were usually unselfish.

She was prompted by kindness, charity, generosity, a concern for the desperate people who needed help.

Some volunteers joined organizations, agencies; others worked alone or in small, informal groups.

They worked for their community (town, city) or for their neighborhood.

Since there is never enough money for all the needs, volunteers undertake the hard task of raising (getting) the necessary funds.

They get good results without wasting any of their resources: they are efficient.

Many volunteers work in hospitals, homes for the <u>mentally ill</u>, and other <u>institutions</u>.

Dorothea Dix, an early volunteer, can be called a <u>pioneer</u> because she was one of the first persons who tried to improve the life of the mentally ill.

Other volunteers <u>devote</u> themselves to other distressed people.

Brand-new volunteers do not conduct <u>board meetings</u> of the heads of their organizations.

They only work, and get a training that is practical, not <u>academic</u> like the knowledge acquired in college.

To <u>discriminate</u> against a person is to treat that person differently, and not as well as other people.

EXERCISES

True or False?

When the statement is completely true or completely false, answer *yes* or *no*. If the statement is only partly true, explain why in a few words.

1. There are thirty-seven million volunteers at work in the United States.

2. The United States is the only country that has volunteers.

3. Some volunteers do not work directly for people.

4. Children too can do useful work.

5. Students help people in jail by bringing them food and other supplies.

6. The American Red Cross was started by one person.

7. Volunteers have always been women because women care more than men for people's needs.

8. The Gray Panthers provide food for old people.

9. The number of volunteers is going down because of recent changes in society.

10. The only people who don't do volunteer work are the poor and the uneducated.

11. Volunteering for a certain type of work is a good way to find out if you'll enjoy a paying job of the same type.

12. Employers are interested in hiring former volunteers, even for important jobs.

13. Volunteers help only good people.

14. All volunteers belong to large organizations like the Pink Ladies.

15. There are still volunteers, but they don't work out of kindness like the old ones.

Vocabulary

1. When you are *translating* a text, you are:
   a. explaining it
   b. copying it
   c. correcting it
   d. rewriting it in a different language

2. A *document* is:
   a. an important paper
   b. a foreign paper
   c. a foreign person
   d. a person suffering from serious physical problems

3. When a group or a meeting is *informal:*
   a. it is not useful
   b. it is not very organized
   c. it is not large
   d. it is not interesting

4. People who are *recycling* old bottles:
   a. are trying to use the glass again
   b. are filling the bottles
   c. are stealing the bottles
   d. are throwing the bottles in the trash

5. The first people who think or undertake something are:
   a. volunteers
   b. pioneers
   c. would-be workers
   d. funds

6. An *unselfish* person:
   a. thinks only of himself
   b. can do a good job without wasting anything
   c. doesn't think only of himself
   d. doesn't have any working experience

7. The person who represents best what most volunteers are like is:
   a. a would-be volunteer
   b. a professional volunteer
   c. a typical volunteer
   d. a coordinated volunteer

8. An old person who needs an *escort* needs:
   a. financial help
   b. someone to accompany her
   c. someone to bring her food
   d. some advice

Synonyms

Read the following sentences aloud, replacing each of the italicized words with the proper word or expression from the list. Some small changes may be necessary in the order of words and in the noun and verb forms.

efficient	available	dilapidated	prompted
to undertake	to retain	to recycle	academic
concern	devoted to	document	desperate
to escort	handful	hard at work	to raise money
community	brand-new		

1. Volunteers are not always comforting the *very unhappy* or *going with* old people to the store or the doctor.

2. A *small group* of women may be repairing a building *in very bad condition* to be used as a club for young people.

3. Or they are *making great efforts* to support a local orchestra. Since no money is *obtainable*, they have to manage *to get the funds* themselves.

4. Others explain the importance of *official papers* to *very new* citizens, and tell them why they should *keep* them carefully.

5. Those who are *deeply caring for* the protection of natural resources spend hours collecting and crushing old bottles that can be *used again*.

6. Others *take up* the hard task of protecting animals, while those with *scholarly* interests work in the local library.

7. All of them are *moved* by a desire to improve life in their *town*.

8. But they are not all *capable of getting the best results for the least cost.*

Word Forms

Complete each of the following sentences with the correct word; be sure to make the necessary changes in the noun and verb forms.

1. *volunteer, to volunteer, voluntary, voluntarily*

   a. The first American fire departments were not staffed with professionals, but with citizens who _____ to fight fires in their community.
   b. They didn't need paid members because there were enough _____ to do the job.
   c. Some fire departments are still _____ nonprofit associations.
   d. They are formed of citizens who _____ fight fires in their town.

2. *document, to document, documentary*

   a. _____ are not only important papers, but papers providing information, or papers used to prove something.

b. If you say that you graduated from a school, for example, you may be asked to _____ your claim, by showing your graduation papers.

c. Last night, the television showed a _____ film on the life of the Eskimos.

3. *efficiency, efficient, efficiently*

a. An _____ car is one that doesn't use much gasoline.

b. Some cars, which are not very attractive, are popular because of their _____ .

c. Some agencies would get better results if they were run more _____ .

4. *mistake, to be mistaken, mistakenly*

a. The newspapers _____ announced that the recycling center would collect old magazines.

b. We thought that the center was buying old bottles, but we were _____ .

c. The person who translated this text made several _____ .

5. *event, eventual, eventually*

a. An _____ is something, usually rather important, that has happened.

b. Some volunteers make a list of their volunteer experiences to show an _____ *(possible, future)* employer what they can do.

c. Even if they don't need it immediately, it may _____ *(finally)* be useful.

6. *boredom, to bore, boring*

a. It can be very _____ to do the same work all the time.

b. Office workers often complain of _____ .

c. Some volunteers visit old people who are alone at home and _____ because they have nothing to do.

7. *formality, formal/informal, informally*

a. A diplomat has to go to many _____ ceremonies, elegant and strictly organized.

b. There is less _____ in private life.

c. Most people prefer _____ gatherings, without ceremony or rules.

d. Although there was no official announcement, we were told _____ that the government would provide some funds for the project.

8. *relief, to relieve, relieved*

a. We are _____ to know that the accident was not serious.

b. We learned with great _____ that nobody was wounded.

c. The news _____ us of our anxiety.

Prepositions

Read the following sentences aloud, supplying the missing preposition.

against   as   at   by   for   in   into   of   on   to   with

1. _____ some big cities, young lawyers give free legal advice _____ the poor who need such advice but have no money _____ it.

2. They devote many hours _____ these people's problems _____ the evening, although they are usually hard _____ work all day, and don't have much time _____ their hands.

3. Their reason _____ giving their service is unselfish. _____ the other hand, their volunteer work provides them _____ experience _____ their future career.

4. A number _____ French volunteers belong _____ Auxilia, an agency launched _____ 1926. Auxilia is devoted _____ the education _____ shut-in children.

5. Shut-in children are those forced _____ their handicap or disease to remain _____ the hospital, or _____ their bed _____ home.

6. The volunteers of Auxilia have a program _____ lessons prepared _____ these children. They send or deliver the homework _____ the children.

7. The members _____ Auxilia were aware _____ the needs _____ other people _____ an education: _____ 1963, they started to help jail inmates.

8. Prisoners are anxious to learn because they'll have to compete _____ jobs when they leave jail; they know that many employers will discriminate _____ them.

9. All the shut-ins regard the volunteers _____ their friends.

10. Auxilia has been recently turned _____ a government agency using television. Voluntary and professional teachers give televised lessons _____ shut-ins.

Out Of . . .

The expression *out of* has several meanings, three of which are shown in the following examples.

Examples: The agency is *out of funds:* the agency has no funds left.
Miss Barton paid *out of her own money*: she paid with her own money.
She did it *out of kindness:* she did it because she was kind.

A. Place each of the following expressions in the sentence to which it belongs.

out of danger   out of date   out of work   out of season
out of patience   out of sight   out of office

1. George is looking for a job; he has been _____ for several months.

2. She was _____ and she spanked the children.

3. George has been very sick, but the doctor says that he now is _____ .

4. Strawberries are very expensive now because they are _____ .

5. Are you sure that the figures you are giving are not old and _____ ?

6. We stood on the sidewalk and watched their car until it was _____ .

7. George used to be mayor of the town; but he is now _____ .

B. Things can be done *out of* anger, pity, curiosity, boredom, fear, gratitude, revenge, kindness, admiration, and many other feelings. How would you complete the following sentences?

1. A person might kill out of _____ .

2. People ask questions out of _____ .

3. People become vandals out of _____ .

4. You might want to become someone's friend out of _____ .

Asking Questions

Many questions can be asked about one single statement.

Example: About fifty thousand volunteers are helping lonely old people in the United States today, by feeding them, escorting them, and telephoning them.
Who is helping old people?
Whom are they helping? (Whom are the volunteers helping?)
How many volunteers are doing this?
Which old people are they helping?
What are they doing for them?
When are they helping them?
Where are they helping them? (Where is this happening?)
In what country are those volunteers? (In what country are they helping them?)
How are they helping them?
Who is helping whom?

See how many questions you can think of asking about the following statements.

1. Clara Barton was a forty-year-old woman who bought supplies needed by soldiers in army hospitals during the Civil War.

2. Three or four Travelers' Aid volunteers wait every day in railroad stations to help travelers with problems of any kind.

3. Between 1870 and 1873 Clara Barton lived in Europe and helped establish hospitals for wounded soldiers during the war between France and Germany.

4. In February 1865, Clara Barton and Dorothea Dix met by chance in a town named Junction.

5. A former jail inmate spends his free time visiting prisons and hospitals; he talks to young drug users because he wants to help them avoid the mistakes that he made when he was their age.

Informal Questions Ending with a Preposition

In a formal question (usually in a written text), the preposition must be placed before the question word, such as *which, whom,* or *where.*
      From whom did you hear that story?
In informal conversation, the preposition is placed at the end of the question:
      Whom did you hear that story *from?*

Ask the informal questions that would be answered with the following statements. Be sure to use the proper question word (*which, whom,* or *where*) and the correct pronoun.

Examples: It is like any other job. *What is it like?*
            He looks like his brother. *Whom does he look like?*
            She is working for an agency. *Whom is she working for?*
            They came from all over the world. *Where did they come from?*

1. It tastes like honey.

2. They raise money for a local orchestra.

3. We are working with the nurses.

4. They translate the information for a group of tourists.

5. She was writing with a red pencil.

6. I am cooking for senior citizens. (Use *you* in the question.)

7. He was thinking of his new job.

8. We are working with a group of youngsters.

9. She paid with her own money.

10. They deliver the meals to twenty old people.

11. She came from New England.

12. It was just like a large hospital.

13. It sounds like a call for help.

Topics for Discussion or Composition

1. Have you seen any volunteers at work? What were they doing? Did it help?

2. Have you ever worked as a volunteer? What were you doing?

1. Have you seen any volunteers at work? What were they doing? Did it help?

4. What people most need to be helped: the elderly, the young, the poor, the sick, the handicapped, the uneducated, or any other group of people? What should we do for them?

5. Were you surprised by some of the facts mentioned in the article? Which ones?

6. Have you noticed something that could be done in your community, in your neighborhood? What is it?

7. In France, a group of volunteer women visit the women's section of the hospitals and offer some beauty treatment to the patients, particularly to women whose faces have been damaged by their illness or their accident. Do you think that this is a wise or a foolish idea? Why?

8. Do you know what the Red Cross does?

9. Do you think that other materials could be recycled besides glass, aluminum, paper, and rags?

10. Do you know of any man or woman in another country who, like Clara Barton, started a volunteer program?

11. In what way do you think the volunteer "grandparents" are helping the young people that they adopt as "grandchildren"? Do you think their help is important?

12. In some cities, young people have volunteered to become the "grandchildren" of lonely senior citizens. How can they help the old people? Is it easy to help them? Would you like to do it?

For Composition Only

A friend of yours doesn't know anything about volunteers (who they are, what they do, why they do it, etc.) Write a summary of what you would tell your friend.

The New Breed
of Parents

FOR MANY YOUNG people, the late 1960s* was a period of revolt against the moral values that had been the strength and pride of the past generations[1]. They didn't want to be hardworking and thrifty°, as their ancestors had been. They rejected the idea that duty must come before pleasure, and that individuals must make sacrifices when it is necessary for the good of their children or of their community. They condemned patriotism° as the cause of wars, and rejected all forms of authority—whether in government, organized religion, school, or family. All these narrow ideas, they declared, were things of the past and had always been wrong anyway.

°saving money

°love of one's country

It was a distressing time for their elders. Previously happy parents found themselves scorned by their young rebels, who accused them of being too concerned with money and too anxious to impress the neighbors. "True success," the young people explained, "is not a matter of money or position. It's a matter of self-fulfillment. And self-fulfillment consists of reaching one's goals and achieving happiness in one's own way without paying attention to rules, duties, or the opinions of others. We do have a duty to ourselves that is more important than duty to others, even to our own children."

Most parents found it hard to accept their children's attitude. They themselves had been brought up to respect traditional° values; they had also learned to respect money because it was scarce during their teen-age years. They had married in the late 1930s or early 1940s*, at a time when it was explained again and again that an unhappy childhood produces emotionally disturbed adults. A married couple's first duty, therefore, was to think of their children's happiness. If the parents felt bored and unsatisfied, they didn't dare admit it: it was not done*. On the other hand, while Mom and Dad were making sacrifices, they expected their children to obey the rules of "nice" behavior, and to grow up into adults that parents can be proud of. These were precisely the ideas that the young rebels of the 1960s rejected.

°followed for a long time

But rebels grow older like everyone else. The children who were preaching self-fulfillment to their parents are now parents themselves. Recently, a large food company decided that it would be good for them to know what this new breed° of parents ate, how they lived and, incidentally°, how they were raising their children. What values were they teaching them? A survey° was made of 1230 families with children under the age of thirteen. The researchers found that fifty-seven percent of the parents in that group were traditionalists°, while forty-three percent belonged to the New Breed. The results of the survey were not only interesting but rather surprising.

°type, sort

°as a less important fact

°study

°those who are respectful of old customs

[1] A generation includes all the people who are about the same age. One counts three generations per century. In a family, grandparents, parents and children represent three generations. Ancestors are the members of the family who lived a long time ago.

emerge . . .   come out of

children

more . . .   less stiff
pushed, forced

as could be said in advance

The first fact to emerge from° the study was that the New Breed parents had not changed their views about family life. Although they loved their children, they were not centering their lives around them as had been considered proper in the past. They were still determined to pay as much attention to their own needs as to the needs of their offspring°; and they had explained to the children that parents had a right to enjoy themselves and to have their own interests. On the other hand, they were willing to* grant the children the same freedom that they demanded for themselves. They treated them like adults. And they claimed that they didn't expect their children to make sacrifices for them later.

The result was a more relaxed° family, in which the young people felt equal to the adults. They were not pressured° to get good marks at school to make their parents proud, and they knew that they would be free to choose their own studies and later their own career. Obviously, the New Breed was still believing in individual freedom.

But when it came to* teaching moral values, the modern parents seemed unwilling to pass on* their revolutionary opinions to their children. Maybe they were not so sure any more of having been right. Or perhaps they wanted to prepare the youngsters for life in a society that had not really accepted the new ideas, and that was showing signs of rejecting them to come back to the traditional values. The survey revealed that most of the New Breed parents were teaching their children exactly what they had been taught themselves:

- ☐ The only way to succeed is through hard work.
- ☐ Duty must always come before pleasure.
- ☐ Everyone should save for the future, even if it means doing without something that is desirable now.
- ☐ People in authority know best.
- ☐ One should love and support one's country, right or wrong.

More predictably°, they had also taught their children some of the traditional beliefs that had been acceptable to them during their years of rebellion:

- ☐ It doesn't matter whether you win or lose; what is important is the way you play the game.
- ☐ Most people are honest.
- ☐ Any prejudice² is morally wrong.

What about the young generation? What do they think? According to the survey, there is not much difference between the "modern"

---

² A prejudice is an opinion, generally unfavorable, based on ignorance and misinformation. Some people are prejudiced about other people's race, religion, or nationality.

children and those raised in old-fashioned families. More New Breed
youngsters seem to be willing to see their parents take vacations without
them; and a larger number say that unhappy couples should divorce°
rather than remain together for the sake of the children.

legally end a marriage

Surely the older generation (the parents of the New Breed of
parents) would be amused to learn that their former rebels are now
fighting the same problems and the same doubts that distressed *them*
years ago. Many New Breed parents confess, for instance, that they
find it difficult to communicate with their children about serious questions like drugs, drinking, love, sex, death, or money. And despite their
efforts to be "open" and to treat the young as equals, with understanding and respect, the relationship between the New Breed parents and
their children still doesn't seem perfect; one out of four New Breed
youngsters admits that he would keep from his parents any trouble that
he might have outside.

Some old-fashioned attitudes, however, seem to survive any rebellion. Despite the large number of mothers who work outside the
home and sometimes raise the children alone, all the children, from
both kinds of families, declared that it was "Mom's job" to do the
cooking while Dad earned money for the family. A large majority also
agreed that parents had—definitely°—the right to spank°.

*without doubt / strike on
the buttocks*

IDIOMS AND EXPRESSIONS*

Idiom	Definition
the 1960s	the years between 1960 and 1969
the late 1930s/the late thirties	the years between 1935 and 1939
the early 1940s/the early forties	the years between 1940 and 1945
it was not done	good people were not supposed to do it
to be willing to	to be ready to, though perhaps not eager to
when it came to	when it was a question of
to pass on	to pass to the next person

THE VOCABULARY OF FAMILY LIFE AND VALUES

Parents and their offspring (children)
represent two generations of the same
family.
The parents pass on to the children the
traditions (customs and values) that they
have inherited (received) from their
ancestors.
A traditionalist is a person who likes and
follows the traditional customs and values.
A rebel fights the traditions.

There was a widespread <u>rebellion</u> of the young in the 1960s, particularly among college students.

They <u>rejected</u> <u>patriotism</u> because they said that it led to wars; in their opinion, <u>patriotic</u> people eager to support their own country against others were likely to cause wars.

The rebels also disliked <u>thrift</u>, the careful use of money, which had <u>been</u> the great virtue of their ancestors.

<u>Thrifty</u> people avoid spending money and wasting things.

A <u>survey</u> is a study of a large number of people or facts, aiming to provide a good general view of them.

The conclusions that <u>emerge</u> from such surveys are sometimes <u>predictable</u> (when they could have been <u>predicted</u> in advance), but others are surprising.

Some facts are discovered by chance, <u>incidentally</u>, while the survey is <u>conducted</u> to discover other facts.

<u>Spanking</u> is considered to be an old-fashioned way of punishing a child; modern parents usually think that it is bad to spank a child or hit him in any way.

People <u>relax</u> when they are resting, or when they stop worrying.

EXERCISES

Understanding the Text

1. What did young people revolt against in the 1960s?

2. In what ways did they want to be different from their ancestors?

3. What did they dislike in their parents' way of living?

4. How did the young rebels describe a successful person?

5. Did their attitude sound selfish or selfless?

6. How did their parents feel about money?

7. Was there a good reason for their attitude toward money?

8. Why did they center their lives around the children?

9. Did the young rebels agree with their idea of parenthood?

10. Who made the survey and why?

11. Among the families they studied, did the researchers find a majority of tradition-alists or of New Breed parents?

12. Do New Breed parents pass on to their children their rebellious ideas of the sixties?

13. Why do they teach them traditional values?

14. Do they seem to make family life happy?

15. Are the New Breed parents communicating better with their children than they used to communicate with their own parents?

16. Are the New Breed children completely different from the children from traditionalist families?

Vocabulary

A. 1. When do you feel more *relaxed*, before a test or after a test? Why?

2. What do people do to *impress* their neighbors?

3. Where did your *ancestors* live?

4. How many *generations* are now living in your house?

5. Are you *thrifty*? How?

6. Suppose I give you a bag of candy and say *"Pass them on"*; what will you do?

B. Explain the difference in meaning between the following pairs of sentences.

1. I *want* to do the cooking./I *am willing* to do the cooking.

2. Let's talk about the *preceding* exercise./Let's talk about the *following* exercise.

3. They came here *in 1950*./They came here *in the 1950s*.

4. *Keep* the candy *for* the children./*Keep* the candy *from* the children.

C. 1. A man's *offspring* are:
a. his values
b. his children
c. his duties
d. former members of his family

2. A *prejudice* is:
a. a rebellious youngster
b. a serious problem
c. a custom inherited from one's ancestors
d. a judgment against someone or something

3. Usually, a *traditionalist* is:
a. old-fashioned
b. rebellious
c. very modern
d. distressed

4. "The woman *emerged* from the automobile" means:
a. she was killed by the automobile
b. she came out of the automobile

    c. she sold the automobile
    d. she was tired of the automobile

5. The *values* of the past are:
    a. the valuable objects left by ancestors
    b. important people of the past
    c. stories of the past
    d. beliefs people lived by in the past

Prepositions

Read aloud the following sentences, supplying the missing prepositions.

against   around   for   from   in   like   of   to   with

1. The young people ＿＿＿ the 1960s were ＿＿＿ revolt ＿＿＿ the values ＿＿＿ their grandparents.

2. "We are not ＿＿＿ them," they would say. "We are not concerned ＿＿＿ money, possessions, and financial success."

3. "We are not interested ＿＿＿ following old rules that seem wrong ＿＿＿ us."

4. "We don't have to pay attention ＿＿＿ the opinions ＿＿＿ the neighbors."

5. "We don't belong ＿＿＿ anyone, not even ＿＿＿ our parents."

6. "We don't believe ＿＿＿ living the way they live, or ＿＿＿ choosing a career that would please them more than us."

7. "We have a duty ＿＿＿ ourselves: to live according ＿＿＿ our own abilities and wishes."

8. "We must find our own happiness, which is different ＿＿＿ our parents' notion of happiness."

9. Some people accused the young rebels ＿＿＿ being selfish, lazy, and worthless.

10. But others admired them ＿＿＿ their courage, and ＿＿＿ being so sure ＿＿＿ themselves.

11. "Those youngsters are not selfish," they said. "They are not different ＿＿＿ the young people ＿＿＿ the past."

12. "Their parents centered their lives ＿＿＿ their children because they thought it was their duty; but they, too, dreamed ＿＿＿ freedom."

13. "They did not dare to say so; but this new generation dared to revolt ＿＿＿ those old ideas."

14. "They dared to say aloud what many had thought in secret before them. Their revolt was necessary _____ everybody's happiness."

15. "We should pay attention _____ what they had to say."

16. But some former rebels _____ that generation do not believe _____ their old ideas any more.

17. They are no longer sure _____ having been right.

Word Forms

Complete each of the following sentences with the correct word; be sure to make the necessary changes in the noun and verb forms.

1. *communication, to communicate*

   a. _____ is difficult between two people who do not speak the same language.
   b. Some scientists are trying to _____ with apes and dolphins°.

   c. People who cannot speak _____ with their hands.
   d. We have just received an important _____ from a government official.

2. *prediction, to predict, predictable, predictably*

   a. By looking at the sky in the evening, farmers can often _____ what the weather will be the next day.
   b. Of course, their _____ are not always fulfilled.
   c. The children from old-fashioned families said, _____ , that the mother's job was to take care of the house and to cook.
   d. But the New Breed children's opinion on the same subject was less _____ .

3. *freedom, to free, free, freely*

 a. Children talk more _____ of their problems to their friends than to their parents.
 b. The young rebels wanted independence from their parents and the _____ to do as they pleased.
 c. Modern parents leave their children _____ to choose their own careers.
 d. The government decided to _____ all political prisoners.

4. *equality, to equal, equal, equally*

 a. They love all their children _____ .
 b. The number of working mothers now _____ the number of mothers who stay at home.
 c. Two times five _____ ten.
 d. My grandfather didn't believe that children are _____ to adults.
 e. But he believed in the _____ of men.

5. *definition, to define, definite, definitely*

 a. They told us _____ that they would be here at five.
 b. I would like a very clear, _____ answer.
 c. The young rebels _____ their position very precisely.
 d. Can you give me a _____ of *prejudice?*

6. *value, values, to value, valuable*

 a. A survey of people's way of life can be _____ to food or furniture companies because it gives them an idea of the kind of products these people would buy.
 b. We all have at least one friend whom we _____ more than the others.
 c. Peter's parents didn't have anything of great _____ to give him, except the moral _____ that they had lived by.

Another Way to Say It

Instead of saying: "Charles is poor; but he is very happy," it is possible and perhaps better to say:

> *Although he is poor,* Charles is very happy.
> *Despite his poverty,* Charles is very happy.

Give these two forms for each of the following groups of sentences. The noun to be used in the second form (*despite his poverty*) is provided for the first five sentences.

 1. Your brother is young; but he has enough experience for the job. (youth)

2. Joan tried to explain her ideas; but she could not convince her father. (efforts)

3. My friends are proud of their sons; but they don't talk much about them. (pride in)

4. Jack's father is very rich; but he has always lived simply. (wealth)

5. Lisa believes in freedom; but she doesn't give much to her daughters. (belief in)

6. Our children were young; but they knew what they wanted to do.

7. Carl believes in discipline; but he doesn't approve of spanking.

8. Paul tried; but he couldn't explain what *self-fulfillment* means.

9. Martha is very poor; but she doesn't want any help.

10. Her uncle is rich; but he is very thrifty.

11. George is proud; but he easily admits that he is wrong.

Indirect Speech

Change the sentences to indirect speech, as shown in the example.

Example: He said, "I believe in individual freedom."
He said *that he believed* in individual freedom.

1. The researchers said, "We have surveyed 1230 families."

2. They explained, "These families live in different parts of town."

3. They said, "Most of them are traditionalists."

4. They added, "But they belong to the same generation."

5. They claimed, "We find the results of the survey surprising."

6. They said, "We don't see many differences between the children of the two groups."

7. The New Breed children said, "Our parents treat us as real people and they give us a great deal of freedom."

8. They said, "They teach us to respect authority and work hard."

9. But they admitted, "We keep our personal problems from them."

10. They said, "We cannot discuss drugs and sex with them."

11. They said, "We don't dare do it because we are embarrassed."

12. The parents said, "We want to help the children."

13. But they complained, "We find it difficult to exchange ideas with them."

Topics for Discussion or Composition

1. What do you think of the young people of the 1960s; were they too selfish and lazy, or did they have some good ideas?

2. Do you like their way of raising the children: treating the children like adults but making no sacrifices for them?

3. How would you compare a New Breed family and an old-fashioned family? Use examples if you know families of the two types.

4. Do you think that duty must come before pleasure?

5. Is it true that success is not money or high position? What is success?

6. Should parents sometimes take vacations without their children?

7. Should unhappy couples remain married "just for the children"? What is best for the children?

8. Is happiness possible without money?

9. Do you think that the young rebels were right about patriotism?

10. Do you think that most people are honest? What common examples of honesty or dishonesty can you think of?

11. What do you think of spanking? What are the best ways to correct or punish children?

12. Why is it difficult for parents and children to talk about serious questions such as drugs, money, love, or death? Couldn't parents help their children by discussing these questions?

For Composition Only

1. From what Ann Landers said in her article, do you think that she belongs to the New Breed of parents or to the Old Breed? Explain your answer briefly.

2. Write a brief summary of the main points of the article.

3. Why does the author of this article say that the results of the survey were surprising?

7

WHAT MAKES A MOVIE SUCCESS-FUL ?

GEORGE LUCAS had already directed two films, one of which had been financially successful°, when he got an idea for a third one. A good idea, he thought. But when he offered his new story to the heads of the studio° that had financed his second picture, they refused it.

"Listen," they said, "it's too strange; the public wouldn't like it at all. Don't you know what brings people to the theaters these days? Disasters°, monsters°—the more frightening the better. Show them a good flood, a fire, an earthquake, an airplane in trouble, or a shark° attacking a girl; that's what they want to see. Try to dream up* a fine horror story° and we'll buy it."

"No, George," said his friends. "Your story is not bad; in fact it sounds interesting. But this is not your kind of picture. The people who have seen your other films expect from you something serious, with a strong social message. We are living in an age of anxiety°, and the public is not satisfied with light entertainment anymore. They want to see a realistic film about ordinary people like themselves, struggling with the same problems that they have to face every day—marriage, divorce, children, money, and so on. They like to recognize themselves in the characters°. Find a simple subject, true to life, and be sure to* get first-class actors."

"We are living in an age of anxiety," said others. "People have enough troubles of their own without seeing more on the screen. They go to the movies to be entertained and escape their worries; but they don't want monsters—they need music and laughter. Why don't you make a fine comedy with a lot of popular stars? Or how about* a mystery°—a little different from the rest, perhaps, a little unusual? You'd make a fortune."

Eventually, Lucas sold his story to a studio that had already been successful with "strange" pictures. He spent the next two years writing the script° and many more months choosing his actors. There was no star among them, with the exception of one famous British actor, Sir Alec Guinness. At first, Sir Alec had not been very interested in playing a part in Lucas' film, for it was not his kind of picture. But while reading the script, he found himself turning the pages to find out what was happening next. Pleased by his own reaction° to the story, he agreed to play one of the principal characters.

As soon as the film was shown to the public in the spring of 1977, it became clear that it would be the success of the year. Millions of people of all ages, in all parts of the world, stood in line to see it once, twice, or several times. Young viewers screamed with joy and some audiences applauded° at the end, as if the actors or the director could hear them. The main characters were made into toys and the story retold in books and comics°. The name of the film was *Star Wars*.

been . . . earned much money

company that makes films

Shark

very bad events / strange, frightening beings

horror . . . very frightening story

vague fear

people in a play

story of an unexplained event, often a murder

text for the actors

response, feeling

clapped their hands

stories told in drawings

The story of *Star Wars* takes place* somewhere in space, at an uncertain time. When the action starts, the Good People of a planet are revolting against their masters, the leaders of the evil Galactic Empire, who conquered them by force some time ago. Princess Leia, a leader of the revolt, has just been captured by the chiefs of the Empire, who are very bad villains° indeed. They want to know what she has done with the secret plans that she has stolen from them; those plans could help the Good People to destroy the Empire and bring back freedom and happiness to the world. After many hair-raising adventures, the Princess is saved by the young hero and his advisor (Alec Guinness), assisted by a daring spaceship pilot and an eight-foot ape°, who turns out to be* the copilot. Sir Alec is killed, but the hero gets a medal at the end for his heroic deeds. The real stars of the film are two robots° named Artoo-Deetoo (R2D2) and See-Threepeeo (C3-PO), who share the dangers of the good guys and get in many funny troubles of their own.

evil characters

machines that act like men

One of the most surprising facts about *Star Wars* is that it won the approval of* the critics, who are not always pleased with science-fiction[1] movies. They did enjoy Lucas' film, however; and they praised the director for having made a picture that was exciting without violence, blood, sex, or fear. Most of all they admired the special effects[2], which made the viewers almost believe that they were flying through space with the hero, and that Alec Guinness was fighting the villain with a ray of light. Even the scientists were happy because *Star Wars* did not pretend to know all about the future of humanity; and—unlike many other science-fiction movies—it did not claim to be scientifically correct while presenting situations that would be scientifically impossible.

What makes a movie successful? The skill of the director? The talent or the popularity of the actors? A story that touches the heart of the viewers, or a message that makes them think? If we were to make a list of the films that have attracted the largest audiences in the recent past, we would find a suspense° story about a monstrous shark; two musicals° full of lovely songs, costumes, and stars; the story of a family of lions in Africa; the sad love affair of two college students; and a science-fiction movie showing the world in the year 2001. We could add to the list an old but very famous historical picture about the Civil War, made in 1939 and still shown regularly. All were extremely successful, although it is not certain that the critics would declare them all "good," by which they mean well written, well directed, and well acted.

waiting with fear

stories told with songs and dances

What about *Star Wars?* Why was it such a success? It could not

---

[1] Science-fiction stories are based on future, and often fancy, applications of science. Many science-fiction stories happen in space.

[2] Special effects are the methods used to make believable unreal actions or situations, such as living on distant planets or walking into a mirror.

be because of the actors, who were not well known and who didn't have a chance to display their talent; the story was too shallow to require much acting—Alec Guinness himself had only to look sad and wise at all times. It could not be the originality° of the story, which was the old struggle of Good and Evil with a happy ending. It was not the love scenes—there was hardly a kiss in the whole adventure. And the viewers were not likely to recognize themselves in the characters. But are audiences always eager to see themselves on the screen and to be reminded of their troubles?

newness

With no other ambition than to entertain, *Star Wars* achieved its purpose beautifully. It seems that the millions of people who went to see the film simply shared the director's obvious enjoyment of space adventures and daring young men. Perhaps they loved it because it was an honest escape movie°, light, funny, carefully made. It was rather like a good western[3], full of life, fast action, and suspense; and like a western, it had a beautiful young woman in danger, good guys in white clothes and villains in black—and a happy ending.

escape . . . movie that makes you forget the real world

The story, however, was not really finished, for Lucas had not killed the Great Villain at the end of the film. This wise decision enabled him° to make a sequel° to *Star Wars, The Empire Strikes Back,* which also had a tremendous success.

enabled . . . gave him the possibility / second story on the same subject

---

[3] Westerns are films (or stories) showing life in the American West, usually at the beginning of this century, with cowboys, Indians, sheriffs, lots of horses, and plenty of fighting. The good guys usually wear light-colored hats, while the bad guys' hats are black.

IDIOMS AND EXPRESSIONS*

Idiom	Definition
to dream up	to invent, to create
be sure to	don't fail to
how about . . .? what about . . .?	what do you think of . . . .?
to take place	to occur, to happen
to turn out to be	to happen to be; to be finally found to be
to win the approval of	to receive the approval of; to be approved by

THE VOCABULARY OF FILMS

A studio is a company that finances and produces films (also called motion pictures or movies). The place where films are made is also called a studio.

The director directs actors and actresses by telling them what he wants them to do and what feelings he wants them to express. They don't always agree.

Very famous and popular actors and directors are stars.

The script is the text that the actors must memorize (learn).

The people in the story are its characters.

Guy is a slang word for man or boy. The characters of a story can be good guys or bad guys. The principal good guy is the hero and the principal bad guy is the villain. The good girl is the heroine.

The story has a happy ending when the good people win.

Comedies and musicals are light, amusing films. Musicals include a large number of songs and dances.

They are escape movies because they make the viewers escape (run away from) their own troubles.

In a mystery, something mysterious, usually a murder, has happened; the hero and the police have to find the solution.

A good mystery keeps the audience fearful but very curious to know what will happen next; this feeling of curiosity and fear is suspense.

A film is said to have a social message when it presents a social problem, such as poverty, racial prejudice, or bad family relationships.

Films, plays, dance, and music are entertainment.

Actors, dancers, musicians, and singers are entertainers.

When the public, or audience, think that a show or a speaker is good, they applaud to show their approval.

An original film owes its originality to the fact that it is different from what has been done before.

A comic book is a book in which the stories are told through series of drawings called comics.

Newspapers usually have a whole page of comic strips.

When a story is very successful, the author often makes a sequel, a second story on the same subject.

EXERCISES

Understanding the Text

1. Was *Star Wars* George Lucas' first film?

2. Why could he think that his studio would accept his new story?

3. Did he sell the *Star Wars* idea easily?

4. Did everyone agree on what the public wants to see?

5. What advice did the studio give Lucas?

6. Did he follow this advice?

7. Why did the second studio show more courage than the first one?

8. What kind of actors did Lucas choose for his film?

9. Why did Alec Guinness agree to play a part?

10. Why did the critics admire *Star Wars?*

11. Did scientists like *Star Wars* because it was scientifically correct?

12. Does the public always like the same type of film?

13. Why is *Star Wars* compared to a western?

14. What was original in *Star Wars,* and what was not?

15. Did George Lucas achieve the purpose he had in mind when he made *Star Wars?*

16. Why was Lucas wise not to kill the villain of *Star Wars?*

Summing-up

Together, let's sum up the story of *Star Wars:*

> Where does it take place?
> Who is the heroine? What has she done?
> What happens to her at the beginning of the film?
> Who are the other characters in the story?
> How does it end?
> Is it a happy ending for everyone?

Vocabulary

A. 1. What kind of *disasters* can you think of?

2. What is the difference between a *monster* and a *disaster?*

3. When do you *applaud* a speaker or a politician?

4. Why are some plays and films called *musicals?*

5. What is the difference between the *hero* and the *villain* of a story?

6. Can you name some of the people who work in a *studio?*

B. 1. An *escape movie* is:
   a. a film showing a man escaping from jail
   b. a war story
   c. a film that helps you forget your problems

2. A *comic book* is made of:
   a. jokes
   b. drawings
   c. monsters

3. The *script* of a film or play is:
   a. the text used by the actors
   b. the list of actors in the film
   c. the evil character in the story

4. A *robot* is:
   a. the place where films are made
   b. an entertainer
   c. a machine acting like a man

5. *Suspense* is:
   a. imagination
   b. a feeling of fear and curiosity
   c. a second story on the same subject

6. An idea is *original:*
   a. when it is new
   b. when it is amusing
   c. when it is frightening

Word Forms

Complete each of the following sentences with the correct word; be sure to make the necessary changes in the noun and verb forms.

1. *finance, to finance, financial, financially*

   a. In 1978 Lucas _____ his second film himself.
   b. After the tremendous success of *Star Wars*, his _____ situation was excellent.
   c. Good films are not always _____ successful.
   d. Lucas is not interested in _____ .

2. *entertainment, entertainer, to entertain, entertaining*

   a. The most _____ film we have ever seen was a musical called *My Fair Lady*.
   b. While we were waiting in line, our friends _____ us with funny stories.
   c. _____ are not always famous and wealthy.
   d. There is not much _____ in our little town.

3. *laughter, to laugh, laughing, laughingly*

    a. The children _____ when they see the robots.

    b. George said _____ that his favorite character was the villain.

    c. George has a happy, _____ face.

    d. You don't hear much _____ in that house.

4. *success, to succeed, successful, successfully*

    a. The makers of *Star Wars* _____ represented a spaceship battle in space.

    b. *Love Story* was a very _____ film.

    c. After the _____of the movie, everyone wanted to read the book.

    d. When a movie _____ , other directors always try to copy it.

5. *mystery, mysterious, mysteriously*

    a. Nobody knows what happened; it's a _____ .

    b. At the end of the story, the villain _____ disappears.

    c. The story starts on a remote, _____ planet.

6. *depth, deep, deeply*

    a. Many people say that there is no truth and no _____ in science-fiction novels.

    b. But some scientists are _____ interested in science fiction.

    c. *Star Wars* is a simple, shallow story; it does not pretend to be _____ .

7. *anxiety, anxious, anxiously*

    a. Lucas was waiting _____ to see the reaction of the public to his film.

    b. His _____ was shared by his friends.

    c. They must have been _____ also when the second film came out, not knowing if it would be judged to be as good as the first one.

Synonyms

Read the following text aloud, replacing each of the italicized words with a word or expression from the list. Give the proper form of the nouns and verbs.

to enable to	disaster	with the exception of	original
to applaud	anxiety	to achieve (one's) purpose	monster
to turn out	to display	talent	character
robot	to dream up		

    1. The desert scenes of *Star Wars* were filmed in North Africa; they *happened* to be a true horror story for R2-D2 and C3-PO, the most likable *people in the story*.

    2. There were real men inside the two *man-like machines*.

3. The man inside R2-D2 was not a *strange being* but a very short Englishman named Kenny Baker.

4. Nobody knew at first if Baker had any *special ability* as an actor, for he had never acted before.

5. But he and the man inside C3-PO *showed* much courage and patience.

6. Their costumes were remarkable and *unlike anything done before.*

7. But the people who had *invented* those costumes had made them mostly of metal.

8. If they had planned to cook the two actors inside, they would have *reached their goal.*

9. Under the hot sun of Africa, the two men almost died in their metal suits. Besides, the tops of their costumes didn't *give them the possibility of* seeing where they were going.

10. C3-PO's eyes were covered with gold paint, and R2-D2 had no "windows," *except* two very small holes that didn't show much.

11. He always bumped into C3-PO and made him fall—a *very bad event* for the poor C3, who could never get back on his feet without help.

12. Everyone working on the desert scenes watched the two poor robots with much *fear.* When they managed to finish a scene without trouble, the director and everyone else *clapped their hands.*

Idioms

How about and *what about* mean *what do you think of?* or *what is there to say about?*

Examples: How about making a mystery, George?
What about *Star Wars?*

They are often used to offer an idea, to make a suggestion. In that case they mean *what do you think of?* or *I suggest.*

Examples: What about going to the movies tonight?
How about meeting in front of the theater?
What about inviting George?
How about seven o'clock?

Follow the directions given below, each time using the proper idiom.

how about/what about   be sure to   to turn out (to be)

1. Suggest to the teacher that he or she skip the exercises today.

2. Tell a friend: *"Don't fail* to be on time for the show."

3. Tell him *not to fail* to bring enough money.

4. Suggest to the teacher that he or she tell the class the story of *The Empire Strikes Back*.

5. Say: "The robots *were found* to have the plans."

6. Say: "The ape *was found* to be an excellent pilot and a good guy."

7. Suggest that the class applaud him.

8. Suggest that someone give him a medal.

9. Tell a friend: *"Don't fail* to read some science-fiction books."

10. Say: "Leia *is found* to be a senator of the Empire."

Prepositions

Read aloud the following sentences, supplying the proper preposition.

about	during	from	into	on	with
among	for	in	of	to	

1. Margaret Mitchell lived _____ Atlanta and wrote articles _____ one _____ the local newspapers. In 1926 she got an idea _____ a novel.

2. The story was _____ life in the South _____ the war between the northern and the southern states (1861–65).

3. Part of the story was based _____ real historical facts.

4. She struggled _____ her story _____ several years.

5. When she was satisfied _____ it, she offered her book _____ a New York publisher.

6. The story was full _____ life and different _____ most other novels that were successful then.

7. Mrs. Mitchell waited anxiously _____ the publisher's reaction _____ the story.

8. But he had no doubts _____ the success of the book and he published it.

9. The book, *Gone with the Wind,* was an enormous success; it was made _____ a film _____ 1938.

10. People _____ all ages were interested _____ the making of the picture.

11. They felt so strongly _____ the characters that they chose the actor who was to play the hero. The public couldn't be pleased _____ anyone else.

12. The studio got _____ trouble when they tried to find the actress to play the heroine.

13. Although they tried many famous stars, they couldn't find _____ them a woman who had the beauty and the personality of the heroine.

14. When the film was finally shown, the critics' reaction _____ the picture was as warm as the reaction _____ the public.

15. And the reaction _____ today's viewers is not different _____ the reaction of their parents who saw the picture fifty years ago.

Past Tenses

When describing past events, you use the past perfect tense *(I had walked)* to express an event that took place before another one.

Example: When George Lucas *wrote* (simple past) the story of *Star Wars,* he *had* already *directed* (past perfect) two films.

Read aloud the following sentences, supplying the proper past tense of each verb.

1. Darth Vader _____ (to be) the evil master of the Empire, whose former chief he _____ (to defeat) a long time ago.

2. One day he _____ (to capture) Princess Leia, who _____ (to organize) a revolt of the Good People of the Empire.

3. Vader _____(to want) to learn where Leia _____ (to hide) the plans of the Death Star, Vader's most dangerous weapon.

4. When Vader _____ (to catch) the Princess, she _____ (to give) it already to a good little robot named Artoo Deetoo.

5. Before Vader _____ (to capture) her, Leia _____ (to tell) Artoo Deetoo to take the plans to General Kenobi (Alec Guinness).

6. Vader _____ (to ask) the Princess what she _____ (to do) with the plans.

7. At that time, the robot _____ (to land) already on the planet where Kenobi _____ (to be) living.

8. Kenobi and the robot _____ (to seek) the help of brave young Luke, whose father _____ (to fight) Vader and _____ (to be killed) by him.

9. Saving the Princess _____ (to turn out) to be more difficult than Luke and his friends _____ (to suspect).

10. But they _____ (to succeed).

11. The Princess and the other leaders of the revolt _____ (to thank) Luke for what he _____ (to do).

12. They _____ (can) not thank Kenobi because he _____ (to die) before the victory.

Topics for Discussion or Composition

1. Who has seen *Star Wars?*
   Do you agree that the story is shallow, not original? That the actors do not display their talent?
   Why did you like or dislike *Star Wars?*
   Was *The Empire Strikes Back* as good as *Star Wars?*

2. What is the best film you have ever seen, and why do you think that it was so good?

3. Can you compare American films and films made in other countries? Are the stories different? The acting? Anything else?

4. Why do people go to the movies? To pass time, to laugh, to see a special actor or actress, to learn something, to forget their own life, to dream? Can you think of any other reasons?

5. Are people influenced by what they see in the films—the violence, the clothes, the life style, the language? Do they try to copy what they see?

6. Suppose you think of a good story. What do you have to do before it is seen as a film?

7. Would you like to be an actor or an actress? Why?

8. Should children of any age be allowed to see any film, no matter how violent, how frightening, or how "adult"? At what age would you allow children to see anything they want? Which films would you forbid to younger children?

9. Why do people go to horror movies?
   Because it is the best way to forget real life?
   Because it is fun to be scared?
   Because it makes them appreciate the safety of their own lives?
   Because they enjoy seeing the characters suffer?
   Because they are *not* afraid and find the story funny?
   Are there any other reasons?

10. Do the critics know what makes a good film—or does the public know?

For Composition Only

1. Write the story of a film that you have liked.
2. What film have you particularly liked or disliked? Explain why.

ABOUT HEROES

T HE WORD *hero* can be confusing, for it has several meanings. It is often applied to ordinary people who happen to perform an act of great courage—a fireman who saves someone from a burning house at the risk of his own life, for example. Then, the principal character of a play, a novel, or a film is known as the hero of the story, even if he is not particularly brave. But the heroes and heroines that we are going to consider now constitute a third group. They are the giants, the out-of-the-ordinary* figures whose superiority fills our hearts with admiration and awe; the men and women who give us a high example to follow, a purpose in life, or sometimes just a dream, because they represent the person that we would like to be.

Humanity has always had such heroes. Some have been the saviors or the builders of their country, like George Washington, who gave generations of Americans their model of determination°, selflessness, and honor. Others have been religious leaders or gorgeous women; conquerors, athletes°, or pioneers; characters in novels or revolutionaries; saints, sinners, likable robbers[1], or movie stars. Whatever they did, they were all stars—shining, glorious, showing the way to their followers below. The desire to be worthy of them could bring out the best in* their admirers.

Many articles have appeared in recent years, claiming that there are no more heroes in the Western world. The authors say that, particularly in Europe and North America, the young now refuse to admire anyone; that we are living in a world too well informed, too curious and critical for hero worship. The press, books, and television keep showing us the faults of the public figures who could become today's stars, until we lose faith and start looking for defects in any person who seems worthy of respect. In a neighbor or a statesman°, we try to discover the weaknesses, failures, or ugly motives that are surely hiding behind his noblest actions.

Is it true that we know too much? Were our ancestors lucky to be only partly informed? Those who read the first biographies° of Charlemagne, George Washington, Joan of Arc, or other great men and women of the past were not told that their hero had bad breath or disliked his mother; they only found a descripiton of his great accomplishments and their admiration was strengthened°. In fact, early biographers didn't hesitate to make up* an admirable story or two about their hero. The man who wrote the first biography of Washington, for

firmness of purpose

those who are good at sports

one in a high position in government

written accounts of a person's life

made stronger

---

[1] "Likable robber" is a reference to Robin Hood, a character in English literature who stole from the rich to give to the poor. The other heroes mentioned in this chapter are: Charlemagne, Emperor of the West (742–814); George Washington, founder and first president of the United States (1732–99); and Joan of Arc, a French girl who fought for the liberation of her country and was burned by the enemy at the age of nineteen (1412–31).

instance, invented the cherry tree[2]; he admitted later that there was no truth in it, but he said that it was in character* and that it would give young men a good example to follow. His readers didn't seem to object; the book was reprinted eighty times—a tremendous success in those days.

Modern biographers do not invent such stories; they respect the facts, as indeed they should. But we pay a price for their truthfulness, for in their efforts to show "the whole person," they tell us more than we really need to know about private lives, family secrets, and human weaknesses. The true greatness of a fine man is often forgotten in the display; and people lose not only their admiration for him, but their willingness to trust any other "star" completely.

This shows clearly in the remarks of a group of high-school students near Los Angeles, who were asked whom they admired. "Nobody," said a young man, "because the objects of our early admiration° have been destroyed. People we wanted to believe in have been described to us with all their faults and imperfections; that makes it hard to trust the 'historical' heroes." Another student, a girl, added, "The people we try to imitate are the unknown adults, the noncelebrities in our lives. Instead of dreaming of being like some famous woman somewhere, I want to be like my mom's best friend, whom no one in this room would know. But I know and admire her, and that's enough for me."

The qualities required of a hero vary with the times, and some great figures of a certain period would surprise the people of another generation. Consider the explosion of love and grief that followed the death of John Lennon in December 1980. Few deaths have caused such deep sorrow, such mourning°, in so many countries throughout the history of the world. There is no doubt that Lennon was a hero for his mourners. Why? What had he done that was so remarkable? "John was not just a musician," says one of his admirers. "He had known how to express my generation's feelings in the late 1960s. He was our voice and our guide; he changed with us over the years, always a little ahead of us; he opened new horizons for us and encouraged us to venture farther, to dare. To us he talked of love and peace; he was the big brother we needed in a troubled time." Some of Lennon's admirers may have been aware that he was not perfect; but they chose to ignore his dark side to remain grateful for the positive° contribution he had

the . . . the ones we admired at first

sadness over a death

good, helpful

---

[2] All American children learn the story of the cherry tree: George Washington's father, they are told, called his young son one day and asked him if he knew who had cut down a cherry tree in his garden. "Father," said little George, "I cannot tell a lie; I cut down the cherry tree with my hatchet." According to the biographer, George's father was so pleased with his son's honesty that he did not regret his lost tree. Many cherry pies are eaten in the United States on George Washington's birthday.

made in their lives. There are surely many people who don't consider John Lennon a hero, who in fact have a very low opinion of him. But it is not unusual for one person's hero to be another person's villain. Think of all the leaders, revolutionaries, and conquerors who are deeply respected by one nation, one religious group, or one generation, and despised or hated by others.

Television and films offer many shallow heroes to their young audiences. Many parents are unhappy to see their children's admiration for Superman, Spiderman, or for some extravagant rock singer without ideas or talent. But such heroes do not last very long; and after a few years the growing teen-agers are laughing at these objects of their young admiration. They start looking for better guides. And no matter what they say, they do find them. The student who was wise enough to recognize qualities in her mother's friend has a perfectly good heroine of her own°, and one who is much easier to imitate than George Washington or Clara Barton.

of . . . belonging to her alone

It may be difficult to be a hero in the Western world these days, under the searching eyes of a critical society. But surely excellence has not disappeared completely; there are still individuals who are superior to their fellow men by their wisdom, their courage, or their character. They can be heroes if people are willing to ignore their human imperfections and to admit the respect that their admirable qualities inspire. Heroes are needed everywhere, at any time. It's a sad sky that has no shining stars.

IDIOMS AND EXPRESSIONS*

Idiom	Definition
out of the ordinary	unusual, extraordinary
to bring out the best in	to show or draw out the best qualities of
he brings out the best in his students	*he encourages his students' best qualities*
to make up (a story)	to invent (a story)
in character	agreeing with the character of that person

THE VOCABULARY OF HEROISM

Heroes and heroines are men and women who are in some way superior to ordinary people, by their intelligence, their wisdom, their courage, or the nobility of their character.

They are not always heroic (extremely brave), but they always have great qualities or they accomplish great deeds that inspire our admiration, awe, and respect.

Most heroes are celebrities (famous people), such as: statesmen, who are men in high positions of government (the word is usually used for the best ones, those who show ability and honor); pioneers, who are people who lead the way (like Clara Barton did in the care of victims of wars and disasters), and great athletes, revolutionaries fighting for a noble cause, and famous military or religious leaders.

Their admirers hope to be guided by them; the heroes are their guiding lights. Some admirers discover that the object of their hero worship has faults, weaknesses, and imperfections like all other human beings.

The very young sometimes are impressed by very shallow heroes, real people who have little depth, or characters in comics and television programs.

Modern biographers write truthful biographies; they show the failures of their man as well as his achievements.

However, they usually try to give a positive image of their hero, unless they wrote the book to give a negative one, to show that the man was not good at all.

People who deeply worship their hero mourn his death. But a person doesn't have to be a hero to be mourned by his family and his friends. In some countries, people wear black clothes during the mourning period following a person's death.

EXERCISES

Understanding the Text

1. Why is the word *hero* confusing?

2. What kind of heroes is this essay about?

3. Is it good or bad for an ordinary person to have a hero?

4. Are heroes always real people?

5. In the opinion of authors of recent articles, why has the western world lost its admiration for great men and women?

6. In what way are old biographies different from modern biographies?

7. What is the bad effect of modern biographies?

8. Do the high-school students mentioned in paragraph 6 seem unwilling to have heroes?

9. In what way is the girl student's heroine different from the usual heroines?

10. Why was John Lennon a hero for the generation of the late sixties?

11. Did his admirers believe that he was perfect?

12. Can a man be a hero and a villain at the same time?

13. Why do the young have shallow heroes?

14. The author of the essay doesn't seem to think that those shallow heroes are dangerous. Why?

15. Does the author say that there are no more heroes?

Vocabulary

A. 1. You wear *mourning clothes:*
   a. before noon
   b. when you can't buy better ones
   c. when someone in your family has died
   d. when you stay at home

2. A *biography* is:
   a. someone who writes an account of a person's life
   b. a flaw
   c. a story showing the hero's qualities
   d. a written account of a person's life

3. When a woman shows *determination* in doing what she wants to do:
   a. she is showing understanding
   b. she is showing her inability to do it well
   c. she is showing firmness
   d. she is showing wisdom

4. An *athlete* is:
   a. a great religious leader
   b. a great deed
   c. a person who is good at sports
   d. a critical person

5. "He explains his *motives*" means:
   a. he explains the reasons for his actions
   b. he explains his great deeds
   c. he explains how he acted
   d. he explains his goals

6. A *gorgeous* woman is:
   a. famous
   b. very beautiful
   c. very kind
   d. very courageous

B. *To strengthen* means to make strong, or stronger.

Example: Washington's example made his soldiers' determination *stronger*.
Washington's example <u>strengthened</u> his soldiers' determination.
(Note that *on* in *strong* becomes *en* in *strengthen*.)

To weaken means to make (or to become) weak or weaker.

Example: Lack of sleep made the soldiers *weak*.
Lack of sleep <u>weakened</u> the soldiers.

Change the italicized adjective in each of the following sentences into the corresponding verb, changing the sentences as necessary.

1. This product will make your teeth *white*.

2. In some parts of the world, women make their teeth *black* to be more beautiful.

3. That noise is making (people) *deaf*. (*Drop "people" in the answer.*)

4. Lennon's death made thousands of admirers *sad*.

5. He can't tell a lie because when he lies his face turns *red*.

6. It seems that women always have to make their clothes *shorter* or *longer*.

Word Forms

Complete each of the following sentences with the correct word; be sure to make the necessary changes in the noun and verb forms.

1. *courage, to encourage, courageous, courageously*

    a. Even when they are not fighting enemies or saving people, most heroes are very _____ men and women.
    b. Clara Barton ventured _____ onto the battlefield during the battles in order to find the wounded.
    c. Her example _____ even the soldiers.
    d. And Dorothea Dix needed _____ to move public opinion and state governments.

2. *sin, sinner, to sin, sinful, sinfully*

    a. A person who breaks a religious law is a _____ .
    b. A man _____ when he does something forbidden by his religion.
    c. But people sometimes say, lightly, that it is a _____ to remain in the house on a beautiful day.
    d. It is not really _____ , of course, but it seems unreasonable.
    e. You can also say that a cake is _____ delicious.

3. *example, to exemplify, exemplary*

   a. George's father thought that his son had answered with the most
      _____ honesty.
   b. Washington's biographer has been mentioned in the article to _____
      what early biographers might do.
   c. The cherry tree story is the most famous _____ of a made-up
      biographical story.

4. *nobility, noble, nobly*

   a. We usually reserve the word *statesman* to describe a man who has a high and
      _____ view of government.
   b. He is likely to behave _____ even with his enemies.
   c. Mr. Pomfrey's speech was extremely boring, but we admired the
      _____ of his thoughts.

5. *hesitation, to hesitate, hesitant, hesitantly*

   a. Without _____ the cat climbed to the top of the tree.
   b. We _____ called the firemen and asked them to come and help
      the cat down.
   c. They didn't _____ to climb and save the cat.
   d. The cat was not _____ to scratch the man who took it down.

6. *hero, heroine, heroism, heroic, heroically*

   a. Joan of Arc is France's favorite _____ .
   b. All French schoolchildren learn the story of this _____ girl who
      died at nineteen for her country.
   c. Although she was alone and afraid, she died _____ .
   d. There have been other young _____ in history.
   e. Sometimes they didn't really look remarkable until events forced them to show
      their _____ .

Some, Any, No

Read the following sentences aloud, supplying either *some* (in affirmative statements),
any (in questions and negative statements), or *no* (for *not any*).

1. _____ *(aff.)* men and women become heroes by accomplishing _____ remarkable task that no one has done before.

2. Can you think of _____ heroes of that type?

3. Charles Lindbergh was such a hero; _____ man had crossed the Atlantic alone
in an airplane before him.

4. He had _____ copilot, and his plane was small.

5. He couldn't see very well because the plane had _____ front window.

6. Lindbergh had _____ food and _____ water with him. *(aff.)*

7. Had he done _____ flying before?

8. Yes, he had piloted a mail plane but he had never made _____ flights over the ocean.

9. He had _____ *(neg.)* fear, however.

10. Do you know _____ other person who did the same thing?

11. Amelia Earheart did; _____ *(neg.)* woman had crossed the Atlantic alone before her.

12. It took _____ *(aff.)* courage to do it.

Tag Questions

After making a statement, you sometimes add a tag question to ask if the statement is correct.

Examples: Lindbergh *is* still alive, *isn't he?*
We *could* name many heroes, *couldn't we?*
The students *will* find somebody to admire, *won't they?*
You *have heard* young George's story, *haven't you?*
His father *forgave* him, *didn't he?*

When the statement is affirmative, as in the examples, the tag question is negative. If the verb of the statement is an auxiliary *(to be, to have, can/could, shall, will, would, should),* the question repeats the same auxiliary, in the same tense. In all other cases, the tag question uses the verb *to do,* as in the last example.

1. You have visited Luxembourg, _____ ?

2. The roads there are very well kept, _____ ?

3. And driving is a pleasant way to see the country, _____ ?

4. We had a wonderful time there, _____ ?

5. The people of Luxembourg like to remember their heroes, _____ ?

6. Many of these heroes are men who fought for the country, _____ ?

7. One of them was a blind king, _____ ?

8. You can remember his name, _____ ?

9. We could find it in the dictionary, _____ ?

10. Now that I remember it, I should write it down, _____ ?

11. They told us his name was John, _____ ?

12. He will always be remembered, _____ ?

13. In his last battle, he lost his horse, _____ ?

14. His men helped him find it, _____ ?

15. And he fought very bravely to the end, _____ ?

16. You have visited his grave, _____ ?

17. Newly married couples often go to that grave, _____ ?

18. It's a mark of respect and admiration, _____ ?

19. It brings good luck to touch his statue, _____ ?

20. We touched it, _____ ?

21. You will tell that story to your children, _____ ?

22. They would think you made it up, _____ ?

23. But it's a true story, _____ ?

Topics for Discussion

1. What is a hero, in your opinion?

2. What heroes and heroines can you name?

3. Was John Lennon a hero?

4. Should we know "everything" about public figures like movie stars, leaders, athletes and politicians?

5. What single person do you greatly admire in the present? In the past?

6. At the beginning of each year, *Time* magazine carries on its cover the picture of the man or the woman who "has most influenced world events" in the past year, or who has been the most remarkable person. In a way this is the hero or the heroine of the year. Many readers are angry when *Time* chooses a person who has done something bad. Do you agree with them that the "man of the year" should always be chosen from among the good; or do you agree with *Time* that an evil person can be the year's hero?

7. Do you have a hero in your family or your neighborhood? Why do you admire that person?

8. Do you agree that people need heroes?

9. Have you read a biography or seen a film showing a historical figure's life? Who was the hero or heroine? Why did you like or dislike the book or the film?

10. Would you say that the good guys of *Star Wars* are heroes?

11. Many nations have, in their history, a type of people who are considered heroes, although they are not known individually; for example, the cowboys of westerns could be described as heroes. Do you think they are heroes? Do you know of other "group" heroes?

For Composition Only

1. Write a short summary of the author's main points.

2. What do you think of this article? Explain briefly what you like and what you dislike and give your reasons.

9

a
fish
story

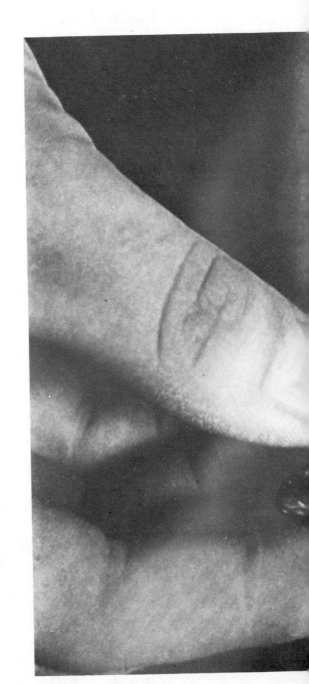

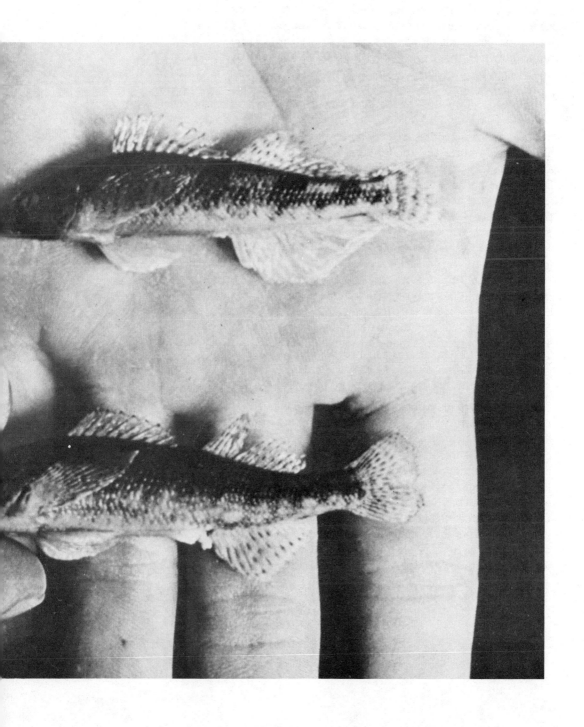

D O YOU LIKE to fish? Even if you do, you will probably never find a snail darter at the end of your line. It doesn't matter; you wouldn't be impressed by your catch anyway. The snail darter is a small fish, three inches long, swift and pretty in the water but totally uninteresting out of it. It eats snails°. The only other remarkable fact about the little fellow is that, until recently, it lived in one place only: the shallow, fast flowing waters of the Little Tennessee River in the south of the United States.

No one had ever objected to the snail darter's choice of home, mainly because nobody knew of the fish's existence. Some one hundred and forty* other kinds of darter are known in North America, all looking so much alike that it takes an expert to* tell them apart*, and then only with difficulty. New kinds are discovered now and then. But no one had ever met the snail darter until a university professor found it in the Little Tennessee in the summer of 1973. The professor promptly gave his fish a scientific name (*Percina tanasi*) and wrote an article about it. Our snail darter was on its way to fame.

Since 1936, the Tennessee Valley Authority[1] had been planning to build a dam° on the Little Tennessee River. The work had been started in 1967. According to the TVA, the dam would provide electricity for twenty thousand families, create a lake for recreation°, and improve flood control in the area. Before 1973 there had been no way of knowing* that the dam would also destroy the snail darter's habitat°. The project, which had already cost around $113 million, was nearly completed when *Percina tanasi* suddenly came to the world's attention*.

Many people, known as *conservationists*, are concerned about the disappearance of all sorts of animals that man either kills or deprives of° their habitat or food. The swift increase of the human population, the search for natural resources like oil, the spread of cities, and big projects such as the Tellico Dam of our story have already destroyed many species° that will never be seen again. Not only the conservationists but many governments are now trying to save from extinction° endangered animals such as the tiger, the whale, the great eagle, the buffalo, and other creatures that are fast disappearing. Laws have been passed to protect them. In 1973, the United States Congress passed the Endangered Species Act, which forbids the planning of projects that would threaten the survival of rare animals and plants.

When they learned that the snail darter was in great danger of disappearing forever, the conservationists alerted° the government, the Department of Justice, and the press. They wanted the Tellico project

building across a river

amusement

natural home

deprives ... keeps from having

types, kinds
disappearance

called to attention, warned

[1] The Tennessee Valley Authority (TVA) is a government agency created in 1933 to build and operate dams on the Tennessee River, in order to bring energy and industries to a very poor area.

110

problem presented to a
   court of law

given up, forgotten

to be stopped immediately. The public, comparing the cost of the dam
to the importance of the fish, followed the story with mixed feelings*.
But the law is the law. The court of justice in charge of the case° had
to admit that the dam was indeed threatening the existence of the snail
darter and that, according to the Endangered Species Act, the Tellico
project must be abandoned°. When TVA appealed to the Supreme
Court², the justices had no choice either: they had to support the lower
court's decision. No dam.

Percina tanasi was safe in its river. Nobody, however, was feeling
really happy about its victory. The conservationists were distressed to
see the act applied for the first time in a case that appeared foolish to
a lot of people. The members of the darter family are so numerous that
the disappearance of one of them could not make much difference*.
It seemed shocking to waste such an enormous amount of money in
order to save a fish that was not even good to eat. The conservationists
were justly afraid to see the public turn against the act and all protective
laws in the future. One of the justices was asking if a reasonable solution

discussions

couldn't be found. In the summer of 1978, after many debates°, Congress decided to make an exception to* the act, and ordered the Tellico
Dam to be completed.

Work was resumed on the project and the dam finished. The snail
darter was promptly forgotten. Actually, the little fish may not have

those against

been the real reason for the battle of the dam. The opponents° of the
project wanted it abandoned because they thought that it was foolish
to flood an area of good farmland, producing eight to twenty-four
million dollars worth of food per year, with a dam that would only give
three million dollars worth of electricity in the same period. Besides,
they pointed out that the region was already receiving plenty of energy
from other dams, that there were other lakes, and that the lovely river
itself was ideal for fishing and boating. On the other hand, TVA was

saying strongly
forty-six-gallon containers

maintaining° that the Tellico Dam was needed for cheap energy and
flood control, and would save yearly half a million barrels° of precious
oil.

Meanwhile, Percina tanasi has been discovering the world. Seven
hundred of the little fish have been moved to another river, which they

producing young fish
for . . . without doubt

seem to find acceptable for snail catching and even for breeding°. In
fifteen years or so the experts will know for sure° whether the fish can
survive in its new home.

It is of course very easy to laugh at the story of the small fish that
endangered the great dam. Was the snail darter worth saving? Was it
worth discovering in the first place? Probably not. But we should

² The Supreme Court is the highest court of justice in the United States. Its eight members
are called *justices* rather than *judges*. The Supreme Court interprets the law. It can
review the decisions of any court in the fifty states whenever those decisions are appealed (protested).

perhaps remember that, until 1928, nobody had ever suspected the common bread mold° of being valuable. Yet the mold was already producing the bacteria-killing substance that we know and use today under the name of penicillin[3].

substance growing on
spoiled food

[3] Bacteria are living organisms too small to be seen with our eyes. In the human body, some bacteria cause diseases. Penicillin is used successfully in the treatment of a large number of diseases.

IDIOMS AND EXPRESSIONS*

Idiom	Definition
some one hundred and forty	about one hundred and forty
it takes an expert to	only an expert can
to tell them apart	to see the difference between them; to tell one from the other
there is no way of knowing	it is impossible to know
to come to someone's attention	to be noticed by someone
came to the world's attention	*was noticed by the world*
mixed feelings	good and bad feelings at the same time
to make a difference	to be important
one could not make much difference	*one was not important; one couldn't change things*
to make an exception to	not to apply in one case
they made an exception to the act	*they didn't apply the act in this case*

THE VOCABULARY OF CONSERVATION

Conservationists believe that animals and plants should be carefully protected.
They point out that many species have already been destroyed.
Many more endangered species will disappear if they are not covered by protective laws.
Whales, for example, are facing extinction.
When animals breed, they produce young. If they cannot breed faster than they are destroyed, the species cannot survive; its survival is impossible.
Some animals disappear because their habitat is destroyed.
The destruction of forests deprives many animals of their food and of their shelter.
Congress passes acts, which become laws, in order to protect rare animals and plants.

THE TENNESSEE VALLEY AUTHORITY

TVA was organized to build and operate dams on the Tennessee River. A dam is a huge construction built to control the flow of the river's water, and so to produce energy.

TVA has built about thirty-five dams.

The people of the Tennessee Valley had been abandoning (leaving) the region because there was no industry to keep them working or give them electricity and energy.

TVA maintains that the new dam will save half a million barrels of oil per year.

The dam will also provide all sorts of recreation (amusement, fun) for the population, such as sailing, boating, fishing, and swimming.

The opponents of the dam wanted to stop its construction, but its supporters maintained that it was essential to the area. There were many debates in Congress and among the public.

EXERCISES

True or False?

When the statement is completely true or completely false, answer *yes* or *no*. If the statement is only partly true, explain why in a few words.

1. The Tellico Dam had to be abandoned to save a very important fish.

2. The snail darter was not known when the dam was started.

3. The fish was discovered by a group of conservationists.

4. There are many darters in the world.

5. Conservationists are people who try to save rare animals and plants from extinction.

6. Unfortunately, governments are not interested in rare animals.

7. The Endangered Species Act forbids the hunting and killing of rare animals.

8. The public wanted to save *Percina tanasi*.

9. The court decided to stop the dam because they thought that the project was useless.

10. The conservationists were not pleased with the decision of the courts.

11. The public found the decision foolish.

12. TVA completed the dam anyway without the permission of the courts or Congress.

13. The snail darter may survive anyway.

14. Since the dam was finished and the fish saved, everybody was happy.

15. The last paragraph shows that some things that seem unimportant may turn out later to be very important.

16. Penicillin is a bacteria produced by bread mold.

Vocabulary

A. **1.** What happens when you *deprive* a snail darter of snails?

2. Sometimes it is impossible *to tell* two brothers *apart*. When?

3. What can *bacteria* do to you?

4. Do fish and birds have the same *habitat?*

5. A friend of yours tells you that he has *mixed feelings* about his new job. Do you understand that he is happy or unhappy about the job?

6. Where can you see some *mold?*

7. What do conservationists want: the *survival* or the *extinction* of animals?

B. **1.** An animal *species* is:
   a. an animal disease
   b. a type of animal
   c. an animal's skin
   d. an animal's shelter

2. Who *debates?*
   a. two persons who agree
   b. a person who speaks well
   c. a bad speaker
   d. two persons who don't agree

3. "The whales are *endangered*" means:
   a. they are in danger of extinction
   b. they are dangerous to man
   c. they are dangerous to other animals
   d. they are breeding too much

4. When you *make an exception to* a rule:
   a. you are adding something to the rule
   b. you use the rule infrequently
   c. you choose not to follow the rule in a special case
   d. you refuse to obey the rule in all cases

5. *"It doesn't make any difference"* means:
   a. it is not long enough
   b. it is not important

    c. it is forbidden
    d. it is not possible

  6. In a court of justice, the *case* is:
    a. the problem presented to the court
    b. the protest of the side that loses
    c. the victim
    d. the decision of the court

Prepositions

Read aloud the following sentences, supplying the missing prepositions.

about	at	by	for	from	in	of	out of	to	under

1. Whales are _____ great danger _____ extinction. This fact came _____ the attention of the world several years ago, but some people have known _____ the problem _____ a long time.

2. Men can't deprive whales _____ their habitat or even _____ their food. But they can kill them _____ profit, for they use their flesh and fat to make lipstick and dog food.

3. One of the sad facts _____ whales is that they don't breed often enough to replace the number _____ whales killed each year.

4. Whales cannot breathe _____ water but they can remain deep _____ the water for a long time. A mother whale pushes her baby's head _____ the water as soon as it is born, to keep it _____ drowning.

5. Many people are concerned _____ the future _____ whales, and are anxious to save them _____ extinction. Whales are protected _____ laws _____ many parts _____ the world.

6. Whales are not afraid _____ man. When they don't feel _____ danger, they come very close _____ boats to look _____ the people _____ them.

Word Forms

Complete each of the following sentences with the correct word; be sure to make the necessary changes in the noun and verb forms.

A. 1. *fish, fishing, fisherman, to fish*
    a. I caught a _____ in the river this morning.
    b. A _____ told me that it was not good to eat.

    c. I enjoy _____ anyway.
    d. Is it forbidden to _____ in the lake?
    e. I never eat _____ .

2. *habitat, inhabitant, to inhabit*
    a. There are thirty thousand _____ in that region.
    b. Maybe we'll communicate some day with the people who _____ other planets.
    c. It is more interesting to see the animals in their own _____ than in a cage.

3. *danger, to endanger, dangerous, dangerously*
    a. That river is _____ because it flows very fast.
    b. Bad brakes _____ the driver's life.
    c. In summer there is always a great _____ of fire in the forests.
    d. The wood is _____ dry.

4. *protection, to protect, protective, protectively*
    a. A growing number of people are eager to _____ the remaining wild animals.
    b. _____ laws have been passed in many countries.
    c. One group is particularly interested in the _____ of whales.
    d. Mother apes put their arms _____ around their young.

5. *threat, to threaten, threatening*
    a. For three years, the question of the snail darter _____ the execution of the Tellico project.
    b. The conservationist said that the dam was a _____ to animal life in the valley.
    c. They told the director of the project, in a _____ voice, that he'd better stop the work.

6. *difference, to differ, different, differently*
    a. When the dam was planned, the situation in the valley was very _____ .
    b. The TVA dams have made a great _____ in the economy of the valley.
    c. The darters do not _____ very much in their appearance.
    d. What _____ does it make?

B. Complete the following sentences with the nouns corresponding to the verbs or adjectives in parentheses.

1. The _____ of the human race seems to be assured. (to survive)

2. From four billion today, it is expected to jump to eight billion in the year 2000—a considerable _____ indeed. (to increase)

3. This population explosion will cause the _____ of many animal species. (extinct)

4. It will also cause the _____ of many plants. (to disappear)

5. With such a population to feed, there will be no _____ . (to choose)

6. The conservationists have a _____ that the _____ of all animals should be protected by the _____ . (to feel; to exist; to govern)

7. The _____ of the snail darter is not likely to last long. (famous)

8. It seems that the _____ of a dam takes a very long time. (to plan)

Articles

Read aloud the following text, supplying the proper article (*a, an, the*) if an article is needed.

IN THE NEWS AGAIN

Do you remember _____ snail darter? _____ little fish, which endangered _____ great Tellico Dam for three years, has been found living happily in _____ stream below _____ dam, where it had never been seen before. _____ experts do not know where _____ fourteen baby darters come from.

Until 1976, _____ fish could only be found in _____ shallow waters of _____ Little Tennessee River, _____ river that flows into _____ Great Tennessee. There are many kinds of _____ darters; since they look alike, it takes _____ expert to know when they find _____ new one.

_____ university professor who found _____ snail darter in 1973 gave it _____ scientific name and wrote _____ article about it. _____ conservationists tried to stop _____ Tellico Dam because _____ $145 million project would turn _____ Little Tennessee River into _____ lake, destroying _____ darters' only known habitat.

Then in 1976, 710 darters were taken to _____ small river called _____ Hiwassee, ten miles below _____ dam. Since then, _____ fish has been doing well in _____ Hiwassee River, but it now seems to do just as well in _____ stream to which it was not brought by _____ man.

This may mean that Mother Nature has guided _____ fish to _____ new habitat when _____ old one was flooded. Or perhaps some of _____ 710 darters didn't like _____ home that mankind had provided for them; or somebody took _____ pail full of fish to _____ stream where it has just been found.

Idioms

Make a different sentence expressing the same idea but including one of the following idioms:

    there is no way of (doing)   it takes . . . to (do)   to tell . . . apart

1. *Only* a mother buffalo finds a baby buffalo pretty.

2. But *it is impossible* to please everybody.

3. When a mother buffalo sees her baby with another young of the same age, can she *tell one from the other?*

4. Whales make all kinds of noises to communicate with each other; but *only* another whale can understand what they say.

5. *It is impossible* to know why this darter likes snails.

6. *Only* a fish expert could get interested in that dull little fish.

7. If you often meet two tigers, it will be easy for you *to tell one from the other;* the markings (stripes) on their faces are different.

8. *It is impossible* to mistake one individual for another.

9. "But," say the eagles, "how can you *tell one of us from the others?"*

10. If an eagle was looking at you, the students in this room, perhaps he could not *tell the difference between you.*

A Review of Irregular Verbs

Read aloud the following story, supplying the past tense (simple past) of the verbs in parentheses.

WOLVES

Several years ago, the Canadian government _____ (to send) a young scientist to the extreme north of the country. His name _____ (to be) Farley Mowat, and his superiors _____ (to tell) him that he _____ (to have) to remain there and observe the wolves of the area for a year or so. They _____ (to want) him to find out whether or not the wolves _____ (to be) killing the other animals of the region as the farmers _____ (to say).

The young man _____ (to fly) to the snow-covered country and _____ (to build) himself a cabin. He _____ (to put) all his belongings

inside and _____ (to get) ready for a long stay. He _____ (to eat)
the food that he had brought and the rabbits that he _____ (to catch).
He _____ (to take) long walks in the woods and on the hills; but mostly
he _____ (to sit) around the cabin, watching a family of wolves.

He _____ (to meet) an Eskimo, who _____ (to stay) with him
for a while. The Eskimo _____ (to say) that he _____ (can) understand the language of the wolves; and it is true that sometimes he _____
(to understand) them. He _____ (to spend) several months with Mowat,
then he _____ (to leave) and _____ (to go) back to his village. The
young scientist _____ (to keep) watching the wolves and _____ (to
become) very fond of his intelligent animal neighbors. He _____ (to
find) them very interesting and _____ (to gather) information about
their habits. Of course the wolves _____ (to see) him also, but apparently
they _____ (to know) that he would not hurt them. They never
_____ (to run) away from him and never _____ (to hurt) him.

Mowat often _____ (to hear) them sing together, as wolves do, and
he even _____ (to make) an effort to sing with them. They _____
(to do) not seem to like his singing very much; at least that's what Mowat
_____ (to think). When time _____ (to come) to go back home,
Farley Mowat _____ (to leave) his four-legged friends with regret and
sadness. He _____ (to write) a book about them, in which he _____
(to tell) the true story of the wolf family that he _____ (to have) observed. The book, entitled *Never Cry Wolf**, _____ (to become) a great
success.

* Farley Mowat, *Never Cry Wolf* (Boston: Atlantic-Little, Brown, & Co., 1963).

Conditional

The following statements are offered to suggest a conditional answer, affirmative or
negative, as shown in the examples. Give one answer to each question. Remember
that the verb in the *if* clause should be the subjunctive of the verb *to be (were)* or
the simple past of any other verb.

Examples: You catch a fish; do you take it home or do you throw it away?
           If I caught a fish, I would take it home.
                          . . . I would throw it away.
                          . . . I would not throw it away.
                          . . . I would give it to a friend.
           You are a journalist; how can you save endangered species?
           If I were a journalist, I couldn't save endangered species.
                          . . . I could tell the public about endangered species.

1. You live near a lake; do you swim, do you fish, do you go sailing?

2. We are in a restaurant; do you order fish or something else?

3. You see a wolf; do you run away, do you try to kill it, do you observe it, do you try to make friends with it?

4. You find Mowat's book in a bookstore; do you buy it?

5. You are a member of Congress; do you support protective laws or do you oppose them?

6. You have snails in your garden; do you eat them, do you kill them, do you leave them?

7. A rare animal is endangered by a project; should the project be abandoned?

8. You can have Mowat's kind of job; do you take it or refuse it? Do you enjoy it?

9. Many different fish are on that table; can you tell their names?

10. You catch a strange fish in a river. What do you do: you throw it back in the water, you show it to an expert, you cook it, you try to find its name, you give it to a cat?

Topics for Discussion or Composition

1. The last lions of India live in a small forest protected by the government. The region is poor and the farmers want to kill the lions and let their cattle feed in the forest. What should the government decide?

2. In the case of the snail darter, was it right to stop the dam or not?

3. Have you read an interesting book about animals, or seen a film or a television show that had to do with animals? Why did you like or dislike it?

4. What kind of recreation should a city provide for young people? For old people?

5. If you have lived in different countries, what recreation facilities did you find there that you particularly enjoyed?

6. Some people refuse to eat meat (although it is not forbidden by their religion), because they say that it is cruel to raise and kill animals for food, and because meat is bad for one's health. What do you think of their ideas? Are you willing to give up meat and fish?

7. Laws passed for good reasons and with good intentions sometimes have surprising, amusing, or shocking results. We have seen what happened when the Endangered Species Act was applied to the case of the snail darter. An anti-pollution law, devised to keep automobiles from polluting (dirtying) the air, forces drivers to use a cleaner kind of gasoline—unleaded (without lead). The result has been to raise

the price of gasoline and the price of cars, which need special devices to burn the treated gasoline.

Do you know any other law that has surprising applications?

What do you think should be done about such laws?

Should the law be obeyed anyway?

Should the law be abolished?

Should exceptions be allowed? Who would decide that the exception should be made?

Should the law be rewritten? How?

8. An "insanity law," passed to protect the truly insane criminals who couldn't understand their own crime (and should therefore be treated for their illness rather than punished), has saved many sane murderers. Their lawyers usually convince the jury that their clients were not "completely normal" at the moment of the crime, that the clients' judgment at the time was "diminished." What do you think of that law:

Should it be kept in order to save the truly insane criminals? What should be done about such criminals?

Should the law be abolished because of the sane murderers who escape justice? What could be done to improve the situation?

For Composition Only

Write briefly the story of the Tellico Dam, giving only the main facts.

10

Creative Justice

THROWING CRIMINALS in jail is an ancient and widespread° method of punishment; but is it a wise one? It does seem reasonable to keep wrongdoers° in a place where they find fewer opportunities to hurt innocent people, and where they might discover that crime doesn't pay. The system has long been considered fair and sound by those who want to see the guilty punished and society protected. Yet the value of this form of justice is now being questioned by the very men° who have to apply it: the judges. The reason, they say, is that prison doesn't do anyone any good.

found in many places

people who do wrong

the... precisely the men

Does it really help society, or the victim, or the victim's family, to put in jail a man who, while drunk at the wheel of his car, has injured or killed another person? It would be more helpful to make the man pay for his victim's medical bills and compensate° him for the bad experience, the loss of working time, and any other problems arising from the accident. If the victim is dead, in most cases his family could use some financial assistance°.

pay, repay

help

The idea of compensation is far from* new: some ancient nations had laws defining° very precisely what should be paid for every offense° and injury. In Babylon, around 2700 B.C., a thief had to give back five times the value of the goods he had stolen; in Rome, centuries later, thieves only paid double. "Good system!" say modern judges, who know what bad effects a prison term can have on a nonviolent first offender°. A young thief who spends time in jail receives there a thorough° education in crime from his fellow prisoners. Willingly or not, he has to associate with tough criminals who will drag him into more serious offenses, more prison terms—a life of repeated wrongdoing that will leave a trail of victims and cost the community a great deal of money; for it is very expensive to put a man on trial* and keep him in jail.

explaining / crime

first... criminal for the first time
complete

Such considerations have caused a number of English and American judges to try other kinds of punishment for "light" criminals, all unpleasant enough to discourage the offenders from repeating their offenses, but safe for them because they are not exposed to dangerous company. They pay for their crime by helping their victims, financially or otherwise, or by doing unpaid labor for their community; they may have to work for the poor or the mentally ill, to clean the streets of their town, collect litter or plant trees, or to do some work for which they are qualified. Or perhaps they take a job and repay their victim out of their salary. This sort of punishment, called an *alternative*° sentence, is applied only to nonviolent criminals who are not likely to be dangerous to the public, such as forgers°, shoplifters°, and drivers who have caused traffic accidents. Alternative sentences are considered particularly good for young offenders. The sentenced criminal has the right to refuse the new type of punishment if he prefers a prison term.

another possible

people who imitate others' handwriting / people who steal goods from a store

Since alternative sentences are not defined by law, it is up to* the judges to find the punishment that fits the crime. They have shown remarkable imagination in applying what they call "creative justice."

A dentist convicted° of killing a motorcyclist while driving drunk has been condemned to fix the teeth of the poor and the elderly at his own expense one day a week for a full year. Another drunk driver (age nineteen) was ordered to work in the emergency room[1] of a hospital once a week for three years, so that he could see for himself* the results of careless driving.

A thief who had stolen some equipment from a farmer had to raise a pig and a calf for his victim. A former city treasurer, guilty of dishonest actions, was put to work raising money for the Red Cross.

A group of teen-agers were sentenced to fix ten times the number of windows that they had smashed "just for fun" one wild evening. Graffiti artists have been made to scrub walls, benches, and other "decorated" places. Other young offenders caught snatching° old ladies' purses have been condemned to paint or repair old people's houses or to work in mental hospitals.

A doctor who had attacked his neighbor during a snowball fight had to give a lecture on the relation between smoking and cancer. A college professor arrested in a protest demonstration was ordered to write a long essay on civil disobedience°; and the president of a film company, who had forged $42,000 worth of checks, had to make a film about the danger of drugs, to be shown in schools. The project cost him $45,000, besides the fine that he had been sentenced to pay.

The judges' creativity is not reserved to individuals only; lawbreaking companies also can receive alternative sentences. They are usually directed to make large contributions to charities or to projects that will benefit their community.

Instead of trying new types of sentences, some judges have explored new ways of using the old ones. They have given prison terms to be served on weekends only, for instance—a sentence that allows married offenders to retain their jobs and to keep their families together. Although the public tends to find the weekend sentences much too light, the offenders do not always agree. Says one, "It's worse than serving one term full time, because it's like going to jail twenty times." But prison personnel object that it is too easy for weekenders to bring drugs and other forbidden goods to the other inmates; they have to be searched carefully and create extra problems and work for the guards.

Alternative sentencing is now practiced in seventeen states and is spreading fast. Judges meet regularly to compare sentences and share their experiences. The federal government has announced that it would provide guidelines° to prevent the courts from giving widely different

proved guilty

pulling violently

civil ... nonviolent refusal
to obey the law

directions, advice

---

[1] The emergency room of a hospital is the part of the hospital where the victims of accidents or cimes are first brought to receive medical care.

sentences for similar offenses. The judges have not welcomed the idea; they feel that it will narrow their choice of sentences and clip the wings of their imagination*.

The supporters of the new justice point out that it presents many advantages. It reduces prison crowding, which has been responsible for much violence and crime among inmates. It saves a great deal of money, and decreases the chances of bad influence and repeated offenses. It also provides some help to the victims, who have always been neglected in the past. Many judges think that alternative sentences may also be beneficial to the offenders themselves, by forcing them to see the effects of their crimes and the people who have suffered from them. The greatest resistance to the new kind of justice comes from the families of victims who have died. Bent on revenge*, many angrily refuse any sort of compensation. They want the criminal locked up° in the *locked . . .* put in jail good old-fashioned way. They believe, reasonably, that the only just punishment is the one that fits the crime. And they fail to understand the purpose of alternative sentencing. What the judges are trying to find is the kind of punishment that will not only be just, but useful to society, by helping the victims and their families, the community, and those offenders who can be reformed. "This," says a "creative" judge, "is true justice."

IDIOMS AND EXPRESSIONS*

Idiom	Definition
far from	hardly, not at all
far from new	*not new at all*
to put a man on trial	to try a man in court
to be up to him	to be his duty, his decision
it is up to the judges	*it is the judges' duty, decision*
to see for himself	to see with his own eyes
he could see for himself the results	*he could see the results with his own eyes*
to clip the wings of the imagination	to keep the imagination within limits (the imagination is compared here to a bird)
to be bent on	to be determined to
bent on revenge	*determined to get revenge*

THE VOCABULARY OF LAW AND JUSTICE

When a person breaks the law, he commits an offense, or a crime.

The criminal may also be called an offender, a wrongdoer (someone who does wrong), or a lawbreaker.

If he is found by the police he is arrested.

Shoplifting and stealing are crimes; a murder is a crime involving the voluntary killing of a person.

If the criminal's crime is serious, he may be locked up immediately.

Then he is tried; at the end of the trial he may be convicted (proved to be guilty).

The judge sentences (or condemns) the convicted criminal to pay a fine; or he sentences him to a prison (jail) term.

A man who steals is a thief.

A shoplifter steals goods in a store, sometimes for fun.

A forger signs checks or other important papers with someone else's name.

Although he is not a murderer, a drunk driver can injure or kill people.

When there are two possible choices, or solutions, they are called alternatives. The alternative sentence is "the other possible" sentence (the first one being the traditional one). One of the alternative sentences might be a prison term; the second alternative often consists in giving a compensation to the victim.

The judges call their new approach *creative justice* because it requires creativity (imagination) to find out the special punishment in every case.

Civil disobedience is an organized refusal to obey the law. It is not violent; but the people who are protesting sometimes demonstrate (display) their feelings by marching in the streets, for example. This action is called a demonstration.

EXERCISES

Understanding the Text

1. Give two good reasons for putting criminals in jail.

2. What seems to prove that jail sentences are wise?

3. Why is it interesting to find out who questions the jail sentences?

4. What is an alternative sentence?

5. According to the judges, what kind of criminals should get alternative sentences?

6. What is bad about putting a wrongdoer in jail?

7. What alternative sentences for drunk drivers can you mention? What can the offender do?

8. How can a poor man compensate his victim (after stealing or destroying something, for example)?

9. Must the offenders accept the alternative sentences?

10. Alternative sentencing is helpful to the criminals who are already in jail. Why?

11. Describe the weekend sentence.

12. Why did the judges dream up the weekend sentence?

13. Who doesn't approve of weekend sentences, and why?

14. Is the idea of compensation a modern one?

15. Why does the government want to provide guidelines?

16. Does everybody approve of alternative sentences?

17. According to the judges, what is the best type of punishment?

Vocabulary

A. 1. It is painful to work in an *emergency room.* Why?

2. When do you need a *dentist?*

3. What do *thieves* do?

4. What is the difference between a *crime* and a *murder?*

5. Someone breaks your window and says, "I will *compensate* you." What does he mean?

6. What is the contrary of *innocent?*

7. If you read in the newspaper that a man was arrested for giving a *forged* check, do you know what the man has done?

B. 1. A *shoplifter*:
   a. snatches old ladies' purses in the street
   b. steals cars
   c. steals goods in a store
   d. enters a house in order to steal

2. An offender is *convicted*:
   a. when he is proven guilty
   b. when he is first taken to jail
   c. when he is given his sentence
   d. when he leaves the jail

3. If there is no *alternative*:
   a. there is no explanation

b. there is no proof
c. there is no victim
d. there is no other possibility

4. A *widespread* opinion is:
    a. a very absurd opinion
    b. an opinion held in the past
    c. an opinion held by many people
    d. a strong opinion

5. If you make a *thorough* study of Roman law, your knowledge will be:
    a. complete
    b. limited
    c. prejudiced
    d. false

Synonyms

Read the following sentences aloud, replacing each of the italicized words with a word or expression from the list. Give the proper form of the nouns and verbs.

victim	fine	bent on (doing)	alternative
shoplifter	to present with	offense	thorough
crime	convicted	to sentence	criminal
arrested	jail	first offender	locked up

1. A judge in the state of Michigan has his own way of discouraging *store thieves* from repeating their *crime.*

2. He *condemns* them to give the *person from whom they stole* a box of candy, a bouquet of flowers, and a letter of apology.

3. "I only do this," he says, "for *new offenders* who are *determined to do* better."

4. Normally the *wrongdoer* who has been *proven guilty* of shoplifting would be condemned to ninety days in *prison* and a one-hundred-dollar *amount to pay.*

5. Most of the judge's offenders prefer the *other possibility.*

6. It embarrasses them to face their victim, but they think it is better than being *put in jail.*

7. If the wrongdoer fails to do his duty, the judge has him *taken by the police.*

8. A man and a woman tried to save money by giving the store manager a sick plant and some cheap candy. The judge gave them a *very complete* lecture on the pleasures of prison life, and doubled the *amount they had to pay.*

Prepositions

Read aloud the following sentences, supplying the proper prepositions.

      as   by   for   from   of   to   with

1. Many lawmakers regard the idea of compensation to the victim _____ good, but far _____ perfect.

2. For one thing, it applies only _____ nonviolent offenders; why not give the same kind of sentences _____ offenders guilty _____ violent crimes also?

3. It would be beneficial _____ them to meet their victim; to see _____ themselves the pain they have caused and the problems arising _____ their actions.

4. The sight may discourage them _____ repeating their crime.

5. The opponents of this idea point out that it would be cruel to expose the victims _____ the presence of the criminal.

6. Most victims would surely refuse to associate _____ the person responsible _____ their misery.

7. It has been tried, however; the meeting was far _____ easy, but the offender said that it had changed his life.

Word Forms

Complete each of the following sentences with the correct word; be sure to make the necessary changes in the noun and verb forms.

1. *conviction, convict, to convict, convicted*

   a. An automobile seller was _____ of selling cars that had no pollution-control equipment.
   b. The judge decided to _____ the man; he sentenced him to one hundred hours of work for an agency devoted to the protection of nature.
   c. Everyone agreed that it was a reasonable _____ .
   d. A man sentenced to prison is often called a _____ .

2. *wrongdoer, wrongdoing, to do wrong/wrong, to wrong*

   a. The judges say that anyone who _____ should pay for it.
   b. But a _____ is not always a tough criminal.
   c. And the judges do not like to see them pushed into more _____ by the truly bad people in the prison.
   d. Some people cannot tell right from _____ .
   e. Offenders are never happy to meet the person whom they have _____ .

3. *crime, criminal, criminal*

  a. A murder is a _____ involving the killing of a human being.
  b. The collection of _____ laws and civil laws is called a *code*.
  c. By law every _____ must have a defender.

4. *offense, offender, to offend, offensive*

  a. He is very unpleasant and he _____ many people.
  b. His way of speaking is particularly _____ .
  c. The _____ was put on trial.
  d. Since this was his first _____ he received a light sentence.

5. *assistance, assistant, to assist*

  a. Paul needs someone to _____ him with his work.
  b. He should look for an _____ .
  c. But he really doesn't want any _____ .

6. *prison, prisoner, to imprison*

  a. It seems that criminals have been put in _____ since the beginning of times.
  b. In the old times, a man could be _____ a long time for a small offense.
  c. The Red Cross tries to protect the rights of _____ of war.

7. *question, to question, questionable*

  a. I don't think that he is very honest; his way of doing business is _____ .
  b. The judge saw the offender and _____ him.
  c. The judge _____ the truth of the man's answers.
  d. The man refused to answer many of the judge's _____ .

8. *loss, loser, to lose, losing*

  a. Stores _____ a great deal of money through shoplifting.
  b. The death of John Lennon was a great _____ for those who admired his music.
  c. The local police are fighting a _____ battle against the vandals.
  d. A person who is very unlucky is sometimes called a _____ .

It's Up to You

Answer the following questions with: *Yes, it's up to . . .* or *No, it's not up to . . .*
Provide the right pronoun and the right tense of the verb.

Examples: Who chooses the sentence, the judges? Yes, *it's up to them*.
            Will the offender be allowed to refuse? Yes, *it will be up to him*.
            Did the police officer sentence the burglar? No, *it was not up to him*.

1. Who made the decision, you? *Yes,*

2. Who finds the accused guilty, the judge? *No,*

3. Did the victim decide to see her offender? *Yes,*

4. Do we, the victims, choose the compensation? *No,*

5. Can the members of the family accept or refuse the compensation? *Yes,*

6. Did the dentist offer to work for the poor? *No,*

7. Can the companies make any contribution they want? *No,*

8. Who dreams up the punishment, the judge? *Yes,*

9. Did you choose to do this exercise? *No,*

By + Gerund

Answer the following questions with *by + -ing form of verb*. Several possible answers are shown in the example.

Example: How did they punish criminals in the past?
They punished criminals by throwing them into a prison.
                    . . . by locking them up.
                    . . . by putting them in jail.

1. How did you learn about alternative sentences?

2. How can a drunk driver help the person he has injured?

3. How do the judges try to keep the sentences equal for similar crimes?

4. How does the government intend to help them?

5. How does the new justice reduce violence in jails?

6. How could a dentist compensate a man he injured with his car?

7. How could a shoplifter compensate the owner of the store where he stole goods?

8. Suppose two or three young people want to help an old woman living alone. How could they help her?

Combining Sentences

There are many ways to organize the facts that you want to express in a sentence. It can be done by using words such as *who, which, that, when, and, but, because, since, for, therefore,* or *after (doing), before (doing), by (doing),* or a past participle.

Example: Facts:

Peter has been arrested twice for careless driving.
He has decided to be more careful.

Sentences:

Having been arrested twice for careless driving, Peter has decided to be more careful.

Peter, who has been arrested twice for careless driving, has decided to be more careful.

Since he has been arrested twice for careless driving, Peter has decided to be more careful.

Peter has decided to be more careful because he has been arrested twice for careless driving.

After being arrested twice for careless driving, Peter has decided to be more careful.

See how many sentences you can build with the facts provided here.

1. The boys had nothing to do that evening.
   They thought it would be fun to smash some windows.

2. The boys were young and fast runners.
   They were not afraid of being caught.

3. The boys thought that they had not been seen.
   They went back home laughing.

4. A man had recognized them.
   He told the police what they had done.

5. The boys were first offenders.
   They were not sent to jail.

6. The judge listened to their story in silence.
   He decided to give them a lecture.

7. "You broke all the windows," he said finally.
   "You have to repair them."

8. The boys repaired all the windows.
   They were ordered to clean up the playground.

9. The boys promised to behave in the future.
   They were allowed to go home.

Topics for Discussion or Composition

1. Do you think that the new justice is better than the old system? Why?

2. What do you think is the best punishment for a drunk driver who has killed somebody:
    a prison term (how long)?
    a financial compensation to the family of the victim (how much)?
    loss of driving license (for how long)?
    hospital work or any other type of "new justice"?
    any other punishment?

3. What do you think of weekend sentences?

4. If you live in the United States, what do you think of the justice system? Is it too severe? Not severe enough? Too slow? Unfair? Fair? Can you compare it with justice in other countries?

5. Some shoplifters steal because they are mentally ill; others, because they have no money to buy food or other goods that they need. But most shoplifters seem to steal in order to impress their friends with their "courage," or just to have fun. They usually say that the store can afford the loss, or that nobody will notice. Do you feel that this is true? Is shoplifting as bad, or serious, as any other sort of theft? If you were a judge, how would you punish shoplifters?

6. Do you think that the victim of a crime should always receive compensation, either from the criminal or from the state? Or should the victim accept his problem without help, as he would have to accept disease or any other misfortune?

7. Do you think that it is a good idea to make the victim and the offender meet face to face? Why is it good, or bad?

For Composition Only

1. Write an outline of this essay, listing the main points and giving examples.

2. If you were a judge, would you rather give jail sentences or alternative sentences? Why? Give examples of some offenses (possibly offenses that have not been mentioned in the essay) and the sentences that you would give.

3. Do you think that murderers should be condemned to death?

11
salaries

NAT'L. SECRETARIES' DAY
RAISES
NOT ROSES
9 to 5 ORGANIZATION

I N 1979 A WELL-KNOWN ANCHORMAN° signed a five-year contract that assured him a yearly income of one million dollars. That same year, a star baseball player earned $350,000; the president of the United States received $200,000 and a teacher of handicapped children made $11,400. Chuck Ollinger, a hard-working plumber° running his own business* with the help of his wife and son, reached a total of $45,000 for his year's labor.

main TV news announcer

workman who repairs water pipes

Although salaries are likely to vary from year to year, the general picture would remain pretty much the same if we were to consider people's earnings in 1969 or 1989, for the relation between salaries remains fairly constant. If the same teacher is now making° $15,000 a year, the ballplayer may be getting around $400,000 and the plumber has raised his hourly rate. Let's therefore use the 1979 figures provided by the U.S. Census Bureau[1] as a basis of comparison between the salaries of different types of workers. The year's earnings were:

earning

$71,000 for the average surgeon°
 55,000 for the average doctor
 24,000 for the average scientist
 17,000 for the average fireman, police officer,
         and postal employee in a large city
 14,000 for the average teacher
 10,000 to 16,000 for the average secretary
  7,340 for the average actor
  4,900 for the average actress

doctor performing operations

It must be remembered that these figures represent the *average* salary in each profession, and that, while the top person makes a great deal more, the beginner at the bottom of the list has to survive on considerably less. A young lawyer just out of law school would have been offered $18,700 a year for his or her first job in 1979; but the average lawyer's income was $57,000 and a star defense attorney° surely made two or three times as much. Among actors, the average income of $7,340 seems unbelievable when compared with the earnings of the top movie star, who gets about $3 million per picture, plus a percentage° of the profit.

defense ... lawyer defending the accused in court

part

Faced with such enormous variations, people wonder: "What does it mean? Are wages unfair? What sort of rules govern them? Why is it that* a plumber can earn more than a scientist? Why does the average actress get less than the average actor? Do the figures reflect a shortage° of parts for actresses in 1979, or does it mean that women always receive less than men for the same work? Why does an anchorman,

short supply

[1] The U.S. Census Bureau is the government agency that keeps general information on the population of the United States, such as the total number of citizens, the average number of members in a family, and the average wages in each profession.

bears ... has to deal with
experts on money matters

who presents the news to the public, make five times as much as the president of the country, who bears the burden of ° events?''

Economists° and experts on wages have long tried to discover what factors were influencing people's salaries. Most of the factors they listed one or two centuries ago are still important today. One of those is education: college graduates have earned and are still earning more than workers who have only finished high school, and high-school graduates earn more than workers who didn't complete their studies there. The difficulty and length of preparation for a profession also plays a part in the size of the salary. Danger and responsibility make a difference too—the man or woman in charge of a project, the person performing a difficult or dangerous task, the airplane pilot responsible for many human lives, usually get a proper compensation for their pains*.

And yet there are exceptions to those rules. Due to* the needs of modern industry, technicians with no college education are now commanding high salaries, much closer to the college graduates' salaries than they used to be in the past. And there are many jobs in which danger doesn't bring much compensation. Why doesn't a fireman earn more than a postal clerk, for example? And what about the policeman and the coal miner, who risk their lives for a modest salary?

abolish, end

The answer is simple. Actually, salaries are governed by a combination of factors, and three of those factors are powerful enough to cancel° the influence of the others. One of them is known as the law of supply and demand, which says that the value of goods and services is determined by the quantity available compared with the number of possible buyers. If there are more chickens on the market* than people

chickens

wishing to buy them, the price of poultry° goes down. If the number of specialized engineers is much larger than the number of positions

people asking for a job

open to them, the salaries drop even for the most impressive applicants°.

The law of supply and demand also explains the low wages for jobs that attract a large number of workers, either because the work is pleasant, or because it requires no training. It is very tiring to wait on tables*, and dangerous to mine coal, but almost anyone can do it; as a result, miners and waiters count among the most poorly paid of all workers. The lowest wages actually go to waitresses.

The anchorman mentioned at the beginning of the article is one of the fortunate people for whom the law of supply and demand works

systems

particularly well. In his case, two television networks° were competing for his services, because they felt that he had the kind of talent that would attract large audiences. The same reason explains the enormous

payments

fees° of favorite movie stars and athletes*, of great dancers, singers, and artists. Talent, like all rare goods, commands a high price. Actually, true talent is not even necessary; any bad performer will earn a fortune as long as he or she is in demand* by a large public; the demand is

matters

what counts°.

The second powerful factor influencing wages is a modern one: the professions protected by a strong union° receive better salaries than those that are not unionized: construction workers are well paid, and so are plumbers, electricians, and truck drivers. But librarians, who have no union, do not make much money. The case of the librarians brings us to the third factor, which is discrimination. For librarians are not only unprotected by unions, but they are mostly women; and the best paid professions are those employing white male workers. Despite the mighty struggle of recent years to correct the situation, women and members of minority groups are still paid less than white men working at the same jobs. An airline hostess makes less money than the man who cleans the plane between flights, and a nurse earns only half as much as a bus driver.

°organization of workers

At the end of the school year 1979, the young woman who was paid $11,400 a year to teach handicapped children was ready to change professions for a while. Since she had never been able to live on her salary, she had been forced to borrow money that she wanted to repay; she also needed to buy furniture and other things. The only solution to her problem was to seek another kind of job. And perhaps she found one. But even if she has turned to another profession, she might come back later to the children that she loved. For people's choice of work is not determined only by the financial reward that they can expect from it. Some are so strongly attracted by a particular activity (nursing, teaching, painting, or translating ancient languages) that the low salary doesn't discourage them entirely. Other people are drawn by the security of a profession, by the chances of advancement, by the location of the company, the co-workers, the working hours, often by the prestige or the excitement of the work. Surely this type of factor plays some part in the choice of a career. If it didn't, there would be no struggling actors trying to exist on four or five thousand dollars a year—they would all have learned plumbing.

IDIOMS AND EXPRESSIONS*

Idiom	**Definition**
to run his own business	to manage his own business
why is it that . . .?	what explains the fact that . . .?
why is it that a plumber makes so much money?	*what explains why a plumber makes so much money?*

for their pains	for their efforts
due to	because of
on the market	available
there are too many teachers on the market	*there are too many teachers available able*
to wait on tables	to take orders and bring food in a restaurant
to be in demand	to be needed or wanted

THE VOCABULARY OF WORK AND WAGES

A <u>job</u> is an ordinary kind of <u>employment</u>, one that may last only a short time. A <u>position</u> is more important and more lasting.

A person's <u>career</u> is that person's chosen life work.

A <u>profession</u> is any occupation that requires education and special training. Lawyers, doctors (physicians), attorneys, and nurses are <u>professionals</u>.

Electricians and plumbers have a special skill, called a <u>trade</u>. But trade is also the business of buying and selling, done by <u>merchants</u>.

<u>Labor</u> means hard work. <u>Labor unions</u> are associations of workers formed to protect their rights, wages, and labor conditions.

But some professions and businesses are not <u>unionized</u> (organized into unions).

A <u>task</u> is a piece of work or a duty that a person has to do.

<u>Workers</u> receive <u>pay</u> or <u>payment</u> for their work.

For his or her <u>services</u>, a doctor or lawyer receives a <u>fee</u>.

Office workers (<u>employees</u>) receive a <u>salary</u>, while people who are paid by the hour—plumbers, maids—receive <u>wages</u>.

A person's <u>income</u> includes the money regularly received by that person from all sources, such as salary and private fortune.

Some people don't <u>make</u> much money and cannot <u>live on</u> (within) their salary.

A <u>contract</u> is an agreement between two or several persons.

A person who <u>runs a business</u> may be selling <u>goods</u> or providing <u>services</u> (repairing watches, for instance).

When the business is good, it makes a <u>profit</u>: it has money left when all expenses have been paid.

If two people run a business together, each person's <u>percentage</u> of the profits is fifty <u>percent</u>, 50%.

When many people are asking for the same goods, those goods are <u>in demand</u>. An actor in demand <u>commands</u> a high fee.

People and companies <u>compete</u> with each other, each trying to do better than the others. Co-workers compete <u>for advancement</u> to a higher position.

An <u>average</u> person is an ordinary person. But the word has another meaning. If you buy four books for $3, $4, $5, and $12, the <u>average</u> price of your books is $(3+4+5+12) \div 4 = \$6$.

EXERCISES

True or False?

When the statement is completely true or completely false, answer *yes* or *no*. If the statement is only partly true, explain why in a few words.

1. There are a number of people who earn more than the president.

2. It is worthwhile to study the salaries in 1979 because salaries don't vary.

3. Actors make a lot of money.

4. People who do dangerous tasks are well paid.

5. Education is a new factor influencing salaries.

6. Women earn less than men in jobs of the same importance.

7. There is an exception to the preceding rule: in show business (movies, theater), women and men get the same fee for the same kind of work.

8. Technicians are in great demand in the modern world.

9. Librarians were poorly paid until they formed a union.

10. The law of supply and demand says that when there is a large quantity of certain goods available, the price of the goods goes down.

11. A singer doesn't need to be talented to earn a fortune.

12. Teachers of handicapped children are attracted to their profession because it is interesting and well paid.

13. Money is not the only factor that people consider when they are looking for work.

14. Plumbers get good wages; but the plumber at the beginning of the story was making a particularly high salary because he deserved it.

Vocabulary

1. Name three kinds of professional people who might take care of you in a hospital.

2. Suppose you are told that all classes are *cancelled* tomorrow. What do you understand?

3. What's a *poultry farm?*

4. Is it the same *to wait for a table* in a restaurant, and *to wait on a table* in a restaurant?

5. When four people share the profits of a business, what *percentage* does each person get?

6. What kind of professional would you need if you were accused of a murder?

Word Forms

Complete each of the following sentences with the correct word; be sure to make the necessary changes in the noun and verb forms.

1. *comparison, to compare, comparative, comparatively*

   a. After reading the list of salaries, one might say that, _____ , scientists are not very well paid.
   b. It may be discouraging for the president to _____ his income with the earnings of a star baseball player.
   c. But it is interesting to make _____ between salaries.
   d. If a shelter is not very comfortable, but better than surrounding places, it does offer _____ comfort.

2. *consideration, to consider, considerable, considerably*

   a. Paul has given serious _____ to his choice of a career.
   b. After _____ several professions, he chose medicine.
   c. He will earn _____ more than his father, who was a postal clerk.
   d. His father's income was never _____ .

3. *to shorten, short, shortly/ shortage, to be short of*

   a. There is a great _____ of water in this part of the country.
   b. The librarian has left her desk but she will be back _____ .
   c. She is back already; her absence was very _____ .
   d. If you are _____ of paper, you can ask her for a piece or two.
   e. Could you _____ that sentence?

4. *profit, to profit, profitable*

   a. He has made a lot of money; he owns a very _____ business.
   b. His father was a good businessman, and he has _____ from his father's example.
   c. Last year was very bad; we didn't make any _____ .

5. *applicant, application, to apply*

   a. Have many people _____ for this job?
   b. How many _____ have you met?
   c. Did you ask them to fill out an _____ ?

6. *fairness, fair, unfair, fairly*

    a. Carl has no favorite among his employees; he is _____ to all.
    b. He pays them _____ for their work.
    c. They appreciate his _____ .
    d. He says that it is _____ to pay a woman less than a man for the same job.

7. *exception, to except, exceptional, exceptionally*

    a. You can say that people's salaries have always been influenced by the same factors—if you _____ the role of the labor unions, which is a modern factor.
    b. Chuck's business has been _____ good this year.
    c. Actually, most plumbers earn about $20,000 a year; Chuck's high income is _____ .
    d. Doctors usually have a good income; the few who don't are the _____ .

8. *demand, to demand, demanding*

    a. Movie stars have a reputation of being difficult to please and asking for all sorts of services, help, and attention; they are very _____ .
    b. The union _____ an increase in the hourly wages of the workers.
    c. But the union's _____ have not been accepted yet.
    d. It has been said that the president's job was too _____ for one man.

Prepositions

Read aloud the following sentences, supplying the missing prepositions.

    among   as   at   for   from   in   of   on   out of   per   to   with   without

1. Reg's parents wanted him to be a dentist. _____ the beginning, Reg didn't like the idea very much, and he disliked it more and more _____ year _____ year.

2. When he came _____ dental (dentists') school, he agreed to work _____ a while _____ another dentist who was a friend _____ the family.

3. The man was old and had said that he would retire _____ the end _____ that year.

4. Reg knew that there was no shortage _____ patients _____ his community, and that dentists usually have a good income, although there are exceptions _____ the rule; there are unsuccessful men _____ any profession.

5. But faced _____ a lifetime _____ dentistry, Reg decided that no amount _____ money could be a proper compensation _____ his unhappiness.

6. He didn't want to become an expert _____ tooth decay or to tell people which one they should use _____ all the kinds of toothpaste.

7. Despite his long preparation _____ a good career, Reg decided to turn _____ the profession that really attracted him. He wanted to be an actor. Of course, he didn't expect to get $2 million _____ picture _____ the very beginning.

8. But even if he had to live _____ less than $2 million, he thought that, compared _____ dentistry, acting would be an exciting profession.

9. He told his parents that he had found the solution _____ his problem.

10. But he soon found out that there was no shortage _____ young hopeful actors, and that, _____ any experience, he could not compete _____ parts _____ those who had received some training.

11. But Reg was an expert _____ animal calls and bird songs, and he could imitate them. He abandoned his hopes of success _____ a movie actor and turned _____ television.

12. He is now known _____ "The Voice," because he provides the quacking _____ ducks, the roars _____ tigers, and the sounds _____ any animal _____ television commercials.

Idioms

Change the following sentences to express the same idea while using the idiom in parentheses.

Example: Right now everybody wants a raincoat because the rainy season is coming. (in demand)
Raincoats are in demand because the rainy season is coming.

1. There is a teachers' meeting tomorrow morning; several classes are cancelled. (due to)

2. The public wants small automobiles because they don't use much gasoline. (in demand)

3. Nurses, who are well trained and work hard, are not well paid. Why? (Why is it that . . .?)

4. The farmers have lost most of their crops because there has been a shortage of water in the area. (due to)

5. There is no need for that type of engineer, because the plant is closed. (in demand)

6. I am never asked when I know the answer. Why? (Why is it that . . .?)

7. The plane arrived late because there was some bad weather over the ocean. (due to)

8. Peter never keeps a job more than a month. Why? (Why is it that . . .?)

Which and That

Which   is the relative pronoun used to represent a thing, an object, or anything that is not a person, and to add some information about it. It is usually used after a comma, and the whole clause starting with *which* could easily be put in parentheses.
The first factor, which is an old one, is education.
A secretary brought the contracts, which they signed immediately.

That   can represent a person or a thing. It is used to define the person or object so that the reader or listener knows precisely that the speaker is talking about that particular person or object—and no other.
The first factor that was mentioned in the article was education.
The first person that we met in the studio was the new anchorman.

Who   is always used, however, to represent a person subject of the verb.
The first man who came out of the room was the anchorman.

Read the following sentences aloud, replacing the blanks with either *which* or *that*.

1. The factors _____ influence people's salaries were listed in a book by Adam Smith.

2. This book, _____ was published in 1776, is still read today.

3. Some of the factors _____ Smith listed are not important anymore, however.

4. Adam said, for example, "The high salaries _____ actors receive are intended to make them forget the contempt _____ society has for them."

5. Today the stars' fees, _____ are still high, are only repaying their talent.

6. Today's public doesn't feel for its actors the contempt _____ our ancestors felt for theirs.

7. Talent, _____ is a rare gift, doesn't inspire contempt.

8. The book _____ made Adam Smith famous was about the wealth of nations; but the full title _____ Smith chose for his work is much longer.

9. This work, _____ is now two hundred years old, is often quoted by economists.

10. Adam Smith wrote several books before *The Wealth of Nations,* _____ is the most famous one.

A Review of Relative Pronouns

Read the following story aloud, supplying the proper relative pronouns: *who, whom, whose, which,* or *that.*

1. The television news program _____ we watch in the evening is prepared by the anchorman and the team of people _____ help him in that task.

2. That news show, _____ lasts about thirty minutes, takes a whole day of preparation.

3. Early in the morning, the anchorman, _____ has already read several newspapers, drives to his studio, _____ is located all the way across town.

4. The people with _____ he works every day are already there.

5. Bits and pieces of news have already been received from out-of-town departments of the network, _____ employs over one thousand people.

6. The studio has a staff of seventy-four people, _____ boss is Sandy Socolow, a man of about fifty _____ smokes cigars all day long.

7. Socolow and the editors (people in charge of parts of the show) meet the anchorman at ten o'clock to discuss the news items _____ have come from foreign nations.

8. They must choose the most important story, the one _____ the anchorman will present first to the public.

9. At noon, it still seems that the main story is about OPEC (Organization of Petroleum Exporting Countries), _____ members are meeting in Caracas. But the president, _____ they can't ignore, is in Iowa making a speech _____ might be important too.

10. After his lunch, _____ he takes at his desk, the anchorman meets more editors from _____ he collects more news stories.

11. Even the cameraman and the typists _____ work on the show give him small stories _____ seem interesting or amusing to them.

12. The anchorman starts writing the text _____ he will read on the air (on TV).

13. A man _____ had been asked to get information about some cancer research brings his notes, _____ are put on the anchorman's desk.

14. It's three o'clock now; the anchorman has finished his story about the OPEC meeting, _____ he still considers the main event of the day.

15. But Socolow, with _____ the anchorman has another meeting, is impressed by the information _____ he has just received from Iowa. The president, _____ is campaigning, has announced important cuts in the budget (planned expenses of the government).

16. The anchorman, _____ is used to such changes, rewrites his text.

17. Then a piece of news _____ had not seemed important in the morning is now getting bigger. The general manager of the show, to _____ the information has been given, brings it to the anchorman, _____ rewrites his text again. And so it goes until show time.

Topics for Discussion or Composition

1. Have you been surprised by any of the facts (or figures) mentioned in this article? Which ones?

2. Is it more interesting to have a career (the same profession all your life, in one or several different places) or to change jobs often?

3. Is there a type of work or a profession that you would not like? Which one?

4. What do you think of the salary of the president of the United States?

5. Should people in public office—presidents, ministers, congressmen, judges, civil employees—be highly paid? Why?

6. Should parents help their children choose a profession, perhaps by starting the necessary studies for the profession? Should parents try to make their children keep the family business?

7. Have you had a job that you particularly liked, or disliked? What was it?

8. In *your* opinion, why do people choose a particular type of work?

9. Suppose you had to advise a younger person on the choice of a profession.
   Would you advise him (her) to go to college? Why?
   Would you advise him to try several types of work?
   Would you advise him to choose a profession early and stay with it?

10. It is considered to be good for high-school or college students to take a summer job, not only to make money, but also in order to find out what the profession is like when they are "on the inside," and what it is like to be in the "real world" as compared to the sheltered world of school and family life.
    What do you think they learn (or what have *you* learned) from a summer job?

For Composition Only

Make an outline of the factors influencing salaries (factors that push salaries up, and factors that keep them low), giving examples when possible.

JOB

INTERVIEWS

12

HUNTING FOR A job is a painful experience, but one that nearly everyone must endure at least once in a lifetime. Books are published, and magazine articles are written on the subject, all trying to tell the job-seekers what they should do or avoid doing in order to survive and to win the game. They can't calm the nervous applicant (and what applicant is not nervous?), but they do offer some advice that deserves consideration.

To begin with, it is not a good idea to be late. Job interviewers don't think very highly of* the candidate who arrives twenty minutes after the appointed° time, offering no apology, or explaining that he couldn't find the street and that his watch was slow. The wise job-seeker explores the place the day before, to make sure* that he can locate the street, the building, the right floor, and the office in which the interview is to take place; at the same time he looks around to see what the employees are wearing and how they seem to behave at work. Next day he arrives early for the appointment. It does not matter if the employer's secretary recognizes him and mentions his first visit to her boss. On the contrary; the eager fellow can only be regarded as smart, thoughtful, and well organized—three points in his favor* before he has said a word.

Most personnel managers° admit that they know within the first few minutes of the meeting whether or not they want to hire the person to whom they are talking. This is particularly true when their first re-action to the applicant is negative°, when the man or the woman has made a disastrous first impression. But what makes a *good* impression? What counts? Being on time does, as we have seen; then, appearance. It is essential for the candidate to be dressed properly and to look alive—alert°, pleasant, interested. It is also very important to look the interviewer in the eyes because this "eye contact" gives a strong impression of sincerity and openness.

The role of clothes and general appearance in all circumstances of life is so remarkable that it deserves a chapter to itself[1]. For a job interview, the rule is to avoid extreme clothes (eccentric° or too fash-ionable), to be neat, well groomed°, and dressed right for the job involved. It may be all right for a nightclub entertainer to show up* in a sexy dress, but the same costume won't help the aspiring° bank employee. All personnel experts agree: no low-cut dresses, no torn jeans, no dirty shoes, no noisy bracelets, extravagant hairdo, or wild beard. And the men seeking a moderately high position should wear a suit (preferably not brown) and a tie.

A number of other frequent mistakes are regularly mentioned by the experienced interviewers. For instance, applicants should never chew gum or smoke (even after asking for permission) during an

---

agreed upon

personnel... people who hire and fire employees

bad, against

watchful, quick-thinking

strange

well... clean, well dressed

hopeful, would-be

---

[1] See "The Right Message" on page 180.

interview; they should not sit down before being invited to do so; they should not lean on the employer's desk, or pile on the desk purse, papers, glasses, and other belongings. If all this is bad, it is even worse to examine the objects on the desk while the manager is answering the telephone, to listen to the conversation—and perhaps offer a comment afterwards. This is definitely not the time to be witty, to joke, to use slang, or to interrupt the interviewer in mid-sentence. Is all this done? Often enough, apparently, to be worth repeating.

Many candidates waste a good part of their interview explaining why they want the job; the man or woman on the other side of the desk is waiting to hear why the would-be employee could be good for the position and for the company. It is much easier for the applicant to answer such questions if he has come prepared—if he has considered his own qualifications honestly, and if he has gathered information about the organization that he wants to join, its size, its market, its products. He won't have to say vaguely, "I'd really like to work here, somewhere. By the way, what do you make?"

The fact that the applicant has taken the trouble to inform himself proves that he is seriously interested in the job, and in the company. It also enables him to answer wisely the questions that are often asked: "Which of your past jobs did you like best?" "What sort of work do you do best?" or "Describe one of your weaknesses." The job-seeker can then describe the work, the interest, or the "weakness" that might
valuable quality be an asset° in his new occupation.

shy about oneself
praising oneself too much It is a very difficult task to display oneself to a possible employer: one must not be too modest°, since it is essential to show one's good points and experiences. But bragging° doesn't make a very good impression. One thing is certain: interview time is a time for honesty. "Don't lie," says a personnel manager, "don't try to hide past problems and failures, like poor grades in school or a job that you have lost through your fault." The interviewer may already know anyway, and the candidate would be caught lying instead of gaining points for honesty. And perhaps the applicant can present his story in a good light*, explain the circumstances in his favor*—as long as he doesn't make the mistake of accusing his former employer or fellow employees.

The interviewer is not necessarily discouraged by a past failure, if he likes what he sees. He is trying to discover not only the professional worth but also the character of the man or the woman he is meeting. What kind of a person is this? Will the new employee be easy to get along with* or will he cause problems in the company, in the office?
summary of training and
experience The employer doesn't have much time to decide, the information he gets from the résumé° is limited, and many personal questions are illegal. Therefore, he must rely on his own observations of the applicant, his gestures, his manners, what he says and how he says it. Everything counts.

While this examination is taking place, the job-seeker should remember that he too has a right to be curious. It is not dangerous, it is
even recommended to ask some serious questions about the job, the
company, the future; if the questions are intelligent, they will impress
the interviewer favorably. Besides, the applicant needs to find how he
feels about the interviewer, the employees he has seen, and the building
itself. He may conclude that he doesn't want to work there after all.

IDIOMS AND EXPRESSIONS*

Idiom	**Definition**
to think highly of	to have a good opinion of
to make sure	to be certain, to do everything necessary
we will make sure that it is perfect	*we will do everything necessary to make it perfect*
to show up	to appear, to arrive
in a good light	in a way that will create a favorable impression
in his favor	to his advantage, on his side
the circumstances in his favor	*the circumstances on his side, justifying his action*
to be easy to get along with	to be easy to live or work with

THE VOCABULARY OF JOB INTERVIEWS

If you are a job-seeker, you first make an appointment with the head of the company that interests you.

If it's a large company, you may not see the employer; you will be interviewed by the personnel manager, who hires and fires employees and deals with all the questions involving the personnel (the workers).

In a small business, you'd meet the boss himself.

To fire an employee is to discharge him or her from the job.

Applicants (or candidates) are usually nervous (anxious) when they arrive for the interview. If the interview is pleasant, they'll calm down progressively.

The interviewer wants to find the weaknesses and the assets of the aspiring employee.

If the candidate is lively, alert, if he answers the questions honestly, openly, and if he doesn't brag (praise himself too much), he will make a good impression.

A modest person is one who doesn't like to talk about himself and particularly to brag.

A candidate who doesn't behave well will make a negative impression, one that turns the interviewer against him.

Many books are written to advise job-seekers; they usually offer very useful advice.

EXERCISES

Understanding the Text

1. Why was this article, and many others, written about job interviews?

2. A job-seeker can make two bad mistakes before the interview has even started. What are they?

3. Exploring the office building, the bank, or the company before the interview is helpful in many ways. Why is this true?

4. What is considered bad manners during the interview?

5. Can the applicant sit down during the interview?

6. Why is it a waste of time to explain why you want the job?

7. Why is it difficult to talk about yourself during an interview?

8. In what way can you prepare yourself for the interview?

9. What should you do about past mistakes?

10. Why do interviewers want to meet the applicants, instead of just reading their résumés?

11. Can the interviewers get all the information they want by asking questions?

12. What different means does an applicant have to decide whether or not he or she wants the job?

Vocabulary

1. A man is *bragging*:
   a. when he is praising himself
   b. when he is telling the truth
   c. when he is apologizing for what he has done
   d. when he is watchful

2. When an employer is *firing* an employee:
   a. he is giving him a job
   b. he is raising his salary
   c. he is congratulating him
   d. he is telling him to leave the company

3. A *candidate* is:
   a. a person applying for a job
   b. a person who interviews job-seekers

   c. a person who tells the truth
   d. a person who lies about himself

4. An *aspiring* actress is:
   a. a person who hopes to be an actress
   b. a person who used to be an actress
   c. a successful actress
   d. an actress who has a very high opinion of herself

5. Your *assets* are:
   a. your past jobs
   b. your past mistakes
   c. your bad qualities
   d. your valuable qualities

6. A person is *easy to get along with* when he or she:
   a. doesn't walk too fast
   b. doesn't talk too fast
   c. is easy to understand
   d. is easy to live with

7. The person who deals with the employees is:
   a. the personnel manager
   b. the personal manager

8. A question about your own life, your family, or your religion is:
   a. a personnel question
   b. a personal question

Personal/Personnel

Fill the blanks in the following sentences with either *personal* or *personnel*.

1. You should never put your _____ belongings on the employer's desk.

2. Peter is too shy to express his _____ opinions.

3. The company is very generous with its _____ .

4. I forgot some _____ papers on the desk.

5. I would like to see the _____ manager.

6. The company's _____ is always given double pay at Christmas.

7. Sheila is Mr. Bertram's _____ secretary.

8. We always have a picnic in August for the _____ .

Synonyms

Read the following sentences aloud, replacing each of the underlined words with a word or expression from the list. Give the proper form of the nouns and verbs.

to take place	asset	eccentric	negative
modest	to advise	to comment on	advice
neat	failure	to join	illegal
delicate	to examine	appointed	applicant
in . . . favor			

1. Magazines often give *suggestions* to *people who are asking for a job.*

2. First, they say, be sure to arrive at the *indicated* time.

3. If necessary, go the day before to find where the interview will *be held.*

4. Even if you are noticed, your eagerness will be *helpful to you.*

5. The interviewer may have an *unfavorable* reaction to an applicant who doesn't look *clean* or who has a very *extreme* hairdo.

6. It is always bad manners *to look carefully at* the papers on somebody's desk, or to *make remarks on* other people's telephone conversations.

7. If you want *to become a member of* a company, it is a good idea to inform yourself about it.

8. One must display one's *valuable qualities* without being *shy about speaking of them.*

9. One should mention one's *unsuccessful experiences* with honesty.

10. The interviewer cannot ask personal questions because they are *forbidden by law.*

Word Forms

Complete each of the following sentences with the correct word; be sure to make the necessary changes in the noun and verb forms.

1. *pain, to pain, painful, painfully*

   a. Carl suffers from his lack of experience; he is _____ aware of it.
   b. It _____ his parents to see him worry.
   c. He is so shy that it is _____ for him to apply for a job.
   d. Besides, he hurt his back in a car accident and he is often in great _____ .

2. *appearance, to appear, apparent, apparently/to disappear*

   a. I waited for a while, then a secretary _____ .
   b. _____ , her boss had forgotten my appointment.
   c. She was not young, but her _____ was very pleasant.
   d. I could see that she was not expecting me; her surprise was _____ .
   e. After telling me to wait, she _____ as suddenly as she had come.

3. *impression, to impress, impressive, impressively*

   a. Martha made an excellent _____ on the person who interviewed her.
   b. She has a college degree, and _____ experience in her field.
   c. Her assets _____ the interviewer.
   d. She can also describe her achievements very _____ .

4. *weakness, to weaken, weak, weakly*

   a. The candidate had a _____ voice; she could hardly be heard.
   b. She said that she had been sick and that her illness had _____ her.
   c. She stood up _____ .
   d. But she said that she felt better, and that her _____ would pass.

5. *employment, employee, employer, to employ, employable*

   a. The company _____ three hundred workers.
   b. If you are looking for _____ , you should see Mr. Bannister.
   c. Many handicapped persons are _____ because they can do a certain type of work.
   d. She works for a small company, but I don't know the name of her _____ .
   e. It must be a good company; the _____ stay there for a long time.

6. *endurance, to endure, enduring, endurable*

   a. Martha has a toothache, and the pain is hardly _____ .
   b. However, she shows great _____ and doesn't complain.
   c. She has _____ a great deal of pain since her accident last year.
   d. This old house is well built; it will _____ for centuries.
   e. It's a long, hard task; you'll be able to prove your _____ .
   f. The palace is an _____ proof of the architect's genius.

7. *failure, to fail, failing*

   a. Paul had to retire because of his _____ health.
   b. He tried very hard but he _____ to convince us of his honesty.
   c. All his efforts ended in _____ .

Idioms

Change the statements to express exactly the same idea while using one of the following.

to think (very) highly of   to make sure that   to take place   to show up

1. The interview *will be held* at three o'clock.
2. *Be certain that* your clothes are clean and well pressed.
3. And *arrive* (appear) a little before the appointed time.
4. The director *has a good opinion* of people who are early.
5. He *will have a very good opinion of* you.
6. The game *will be played* in the large field.
7. We must *be certain that* everything is ready.
8. Hundreds of fans *will come,* I know.
9. Everybody *has a good opinion of* our team in this town.
10. The director was angry because the candidate *did not come.*
11. He *didn't have a very good opinion of* the other applicants.
12. The meeting was *to be held* in his office.
13. He *had done what he could to be certain that* nobody would disturb them.
14. Maybe the man *will arrive* later?
15. I *don't have a good opinion of* this exercise.

Active/Passive

Although the questions on the right side of this page are in the active voice, they should be answered in the passive voice, as shown in the examples. The text on the left side provides the material for the answers. Be sure to use in the answer the tense of verb (past, present, or future) used in the question.

Text	Questions
Examples: A secretary brought the letters at ten.	Who brought the letters? *They were brought by a secretary.*
The director will sign them soon.	Who will sign them? *They will be signed by the director.*

1. A friend told Peter and his brother that the telephone company had several jobs available.

   Who told Peter and his brothers about the jobs?

2. His family advised Peter to apply for a job.

   Who advised Peter to apply for a job?

3. Someone always tells Peter what to do.

   Who tells Peter what to do?

4. He wrote a résumé with the help of his brother Carl.

   Who helped Peter with his résumé?

5. Carl said that most employers require résumés.

   Who requires résumés?

6. Since Peter doesn't drive, a neighbor took him downtown to the telephone company building.

   Who took Peter downtown?

7. The company had repainted the building recently.

   Who had repainted the building?

8. Peter lost his way, but a young woman helped him to find it.

   Who helped Peter?

9. She said, "My boss will see ten applicants today."

   Who will see the applicants today?

10. "I gave the appointments last week."

    Who gave the appointments?

11. Someone in the next office called her.

    Who called the secretary?

12. The young woman came back and said, "The director expects the other applicants at two."

    At what time does the director expect the other applicants to come?

13. "But he will see you now."

    Who will see Peter now?

14. She said, "I told him that I had forgotten your appointment."

    Who had forgotten the appointment?

15. And so Peter had an interview; but the director didn't hire him.

    Did the director hire Peter?

Sentence Combining: While, Before, After

See what sentences you can make with *while*, *before*, or *after* to express the idea presented by each of the following statements.

Examples: I took my coat off. Then I entered the room.
    Before entering the room, I took my coat off.
    After taking my coat off, I entered the room.

    He smoked a cigarette. At the same time he waited for the manager.
    While waiting for the manager, he smoked a cigarette.
    He smoked a cigarette while waiting for the manager.

1. Paul gathered information about the company. Then he applied for a job.

2. He visited the building. Then he asked for an interview.

3. He visited the offices. At the same time he observed the employees.

4. The manager shook Paul's hand. Then he offered him a chair.

5. He looked at Paul's résumé. At the same time he asked questions.

6. He read the first page. Then he looked up at Paul.

7. The manager read the second page. At the same time he answered the telephone.

8. He described the job. Then he told Paul about the salary.

9. Paul said that he would think about it. Then he would give his answer.

10. Paul felt that he liked the manager. At the same time he was talking to the man.

11. Paul thanked the manager for the interview. Then he left the room.

12. The manager said, "Talk to some employees. Then make your decision."

13. Paul went down the stairs. At the same time he was thinking of the interview.

14. He waited for the bus. At the same time he decided to accept the job.

Topics for Discussion or Composition

1. Is there anything in the text with which you disagree?

2. Have you ever been interviewed? What surprised you? Do you remember an interview that was particularly pleasant or unpleasant? Describe it.

3. If you were interviewing applicants for an office job, what would you find "bad" in a candidate—in his or her clothes, behavior, answers, and explanations?

4. What is the best way to find a job: answering newspapers ads, talking to friends, or applying to many companies? Can you think of any other methods?

5. Suppose you were thinking of working for a company, or in a store. What would you want to know before accepting the job?

6. Would you hire somebody just out of jail?

7. What would you like to be when you reach fifty?

8. How would you describe the perfect boss?

9. What does a good employee do? What does he or she avoid doing? Think about the job, the boss, the other employees, and the company.

10. Describe your present job or any other job that you had in the past.

11. If you have lived in a country other than the United States, do you see some differences in the way an applicant there should behave before or during an interview?

For Composition Only

1. You are getting ready for a job interview. Make two lists, based on this article, of what you must do and must not do before and during the interview.

2. You are getting ready for a job interview. Make an outline of what you want to tell the interviewer about yourself, and what questions you would like to ask him.

3. You are a personnel manager expecting several applicants; make a list of what you want to find about them, either by asking questions or by observation.

13

Working Women

TWO MILLION American women enter the work force every year. The new workers include all ages and backgrounds: teen-agers, college graduates launching their careers, young house-wives anxious to increase the family income, society women in search of prestige or occupation, and older women who have lost their husbands or who cannot stand their empty house after the last child has left. Altogether, more than half the eighty-four million women in the United States are now employed or seeking employment. Al-though most of them are still clinging° to the traditionally "feminine°" jobs (nursing, teaching, and office work), a growing number of pioneers are venturing into other fields. They run businesses; they manage farms; they become astronauts, carpenters, lawyers, truck or taxi drivers, coal miners, jockeys°, or politicians. They join the army or the navy. So far° no woman has become president of the country or secretary of state; but that might happen, as indeed it has happened in other nations.

holding tightly / womanly

riders in horse races / so . . . until now

The tide of working women is sweeping the country, with various consequences, some more obvious or predictable than others. One hardly needs to mention the economic effect of their activities, since more than fifty percent of families are now living on two incomes. But few people would have guessed ten years ago that the entry of women in the working world would affect the development of the suburbs. Yet working women, having little time to waste on commuting° from their office to their kitchen, are taking middle-class families back to the cities that they had deserted in the last twenty years. For the city is the place where most jobs are.

traveling regularly

But the most striking° effect of women's new role is of a social nature. It touches family life, the number and upbringing° of children, the relations between parents and children, and the relations between men and women.

remarkable
raising

It would be pleasant to believe that all young girls in the past got married for romantic° reasons; but the fact is that many of them re-garded marriage as their only chance to gain independence from their parents, to have a provider, or to be assured of a good place in society. A couple of generations ago, an old maid° of twenty-five didn't have much to look forward to*; she was more or less fated to remain with her parents or to live in some relative's home where she would help with the chores° and the children. Not so any more. In the first place, women remain young much longer than they used to, and an unmar-ried woman of twenty-eight or thirty doesn't feel that her life is over. Besides, since she is probably working and supporting herself, she is free to marry only when and if she chooses. As a consequence, today's women tend to marry later in life. They have fewer children—or none at all—if they prefer to devote themselves to their profession. The result is a decline in the birthrate.

having to do with love

old . . . unmarried woman

boring tasks

The new role that women have developed for themselves has transformed family life. Children are raised differently; they spend more time with adults who are not their parents: baby sitters, day-care center personnel, relatives, or neighbors. Whether they gain or lose in the process is a hotly debated question. Some child experts believe that young children must spend all their time with their mother if they are to* grow sound in body and mind. Others maintain that children get more from a mother who spends with them "quality time" (a time of fun and relaxation set aside for* them) rather than hours of forced and unhappy baby-sitting. And many child psychologists° point out that children kept in day-care centers every day are brighter than those raised at home.

students of thoughts and feelings

The children of working mothers are getting an image of their father that is different from the one they would have in another type of family. Their Dad is not a remote person who disappears in the morning and reappears at night to learn how bad they have been and to distribute punishment. He is a familiar parent who might serve breakfast while Mother is getting dressed, who knows how to fix a little girl's hair and how to put shoes on a three year old. He is someone you can talk to, just like Mother. That very fact makes many working mothers feel that they have lost some of their "special" relationship with their children. They are not always the first one to hear the "secrets" any longer; Father may have heard them first, or perhaps a well-loved baby sitter. Or perhaps Mother was not around when her little boy finally managed to keep his bicycle straight, or to swim across the pool. It hurts, says a successful career woman.

The relations between man and wife are changing too. A majority of working women remain in full charge of their home; they come back at night to the cleaning, washing, and cooking that constitutes their second career. But more and more husbands are sharing the burden and willingly taking on* chores that their fathers would have rejected as unmanly°, and as too mysteriously difficult anyway. In such cases, man and wife become equal partners, both working outside, both pushing the vacuum cleaner°. Actually, the number of husbands who do help in that way is much smaller than the number of those who accept the idea in theory*. And when the equal partnership is a fact, it doesn't always work well. The marriage can be destroyed when the wife is more successful in her profession than her husband in his, particularly when she earns more than he does. Sociologists° see in this situation one of the main reasons for the increase in the divorce rate—another reason being the husband's refusal to help with the housework or the care of the children. A third reason could be the growing awareness° of the professional women that she doesn't have to remain married if she is too unhappy.

not fit for a man

students of social behavior

consciousness, knowledge

Among all the changes resulting from the massive° entry of women into the work force, the transformation that has occurred in the women themselves is not the least important. They see themselves in a new light, for they have discovered that they can do just as well as men in any profession. Some of them have gone to the top*: the chief economist of General Motors is a woman, and so is the president of the great film-making company 20th Century Fox. Such successes have given women pride and self-confidence. Of course, the picture is not perfect. In the first place, a very large number of women do not even try to enter "male" professions because they lack the necessary training or because they are not bold enough to venture on new paths. For one woman executive or one woman judge, there are still countless typists and saleswomen who struggle through their day without any sense of victory. Besides, many of their braver sisters, who are daring to compete with men in higher fields, find that male opposition is still strong, and that society is still ready to explain a woman's success by reasons that have nothing to do with her intelligence. Still, the fact remains that women are now free to enter any career that attracts them; the situation has improved, and the tide is not likely to turn back.

large, heavy

Women have gained pride, self-confidence, and independence. Have they gained happiness? Each working woman would have to give her personal answer to that question. Many women are too exhausted by their double career (home and office) to enjoy either one. Many feel guilty about leaving their children to the care of strangers, about neglecting all the small things that nonworking homemakers do for their family and their house. For women, taking a profession involves sacrifices—they have to make a difficult choice. Perhaps the real progress is that the choice exists; in their grandmothers' time, it did not.

IDIOMS AND EXPRESSIONS*

Idiom	Definition
to look forward to	to be eager to
we are looking forward to seeing you	*we are eager to see you*
if they are to	if they are expected or desired to
we must hurry, if we are to finish this before noon	*we must hurry, if we expect to finish this before noon*
to set aside for	to reserve (keep) especially for
they set money aside for their child's education	*they reserve some money especially for their child's education*
to take on	to take charge of, to accept responsibility for
in theory	in thought but not necessarily in fact
they are equal in theory	*they are thought of as equal, but the world does not treat them that way*
to go to the top	to succeed, to get to the highest position

THE VOCABULARY OF WOMEN'S WORK

A woman who takes care of her home and her family is a <u>housewife</u>.

She does the <u>housework</u>, the household <u>chores</u> such as <u>cleaning</u> and <u>cooking</u>, and she <u>raises</u> (<u>brings up</u>) the children.

Other women prefer to work and to become <u>professional</u> women, <u>career women</u>.

If they are successful they might become <u>executives</u> (heads of their organization, with authority and responsibility).

Even elegant and wealthy <u>society women</u> like to have an <u>activity</u>, an occupation.

Husband and working wife share the housework; they share equally in the care and the <u>upbringing</u> of the children. In that sense, they are equal <u>partners</u>. Like her husband, the working wife is a <u>provider</u>, a person who provides money and goods for the family.

Middle-class families used to <u>desert</u> (leave) the cities in order to live outside, in the <u>suburbs</u>. The father had to <u>commute</u> from his home to his place of work every day.

Women, who must get home fast to clean and cook, prefer not to waste their time on <u>commuting</u>.

<u>Psychologists</u>, who study the way people feel and think, say that women have gained confidence since they entered the <u>work force</u>.

<u>Sociologists</u>, who study social behavior and relations between people, say that the <u>rate</u>

of <u>divorces</u> has increased since women's <u>entry</u> in the working world.

The <u>birthrate</u> has declined (gone down) because women marry later in life.

An unmarried woman over twenty-five was sometimes called, unpleasantly, an <u>old maid</u>.

Some women got married for practical reasons, others for <u>romantic</u> reasons.

Women have chosen a new role (function) for themselves. Those who choose to <u>devote themselves</u> (give all their attention) to their career must leave their children to a baby sitter or to a <u>day-care center</u> where the children play, sleep, and eat under the care of the personnel.

EXERCISES

Understanding the Text

1. What percentage of American women are working?

2. Is it true that no woman has ever been president or secretary of state of her country?

3. Do only poor women work?

4. Why are some middle-class families moving back to the cities?

5. Are there many families in the United States where the husband and the wife are both working?

6. Why did young women have to marry in the past?

7. Is it different now?

8. Why is the birthrate declining?

9. What is new in the way children are raised?

10. Do day-care centers seem to be good or bad for children?

11. What is *quality time* for mothers and children?

12. Why is the father likely to be closer to his children when his wife works?

13. When are man and wife "equal partners"?

14. Is this always good?

15. Have women gained more than money by going to work?

16. What reasons do working women have to be unhappy about their professional life?

17. What reasons do they have to be unhappy about their family life?

18. Has no progress been made, then?

Vocabulary

1. What does a *jockey* do?

2. Are *psychologists* and *sociologists* interested in the same aspects of human life?

3. Suppose a man is described as *massive,* how do you see him?

4. Do *astronauts* build spaceships?

5. What is the difference between an *old maid* and an old servant?

6. What is the difference between a *day-care center* and a school?

7. If a child is *clinging* to his mother's hand, does it mean that he is holding it?

8. Would you say that the text we have just read is a *romantic* story?

Synonyms

Read aloud the following sentences, replacing each italicized word or expression with the most appropriate word from the list. Be sure to make all necessary changes in nouns and verbs.

provider	feminine	bringing up	salary
anxious	increasing	ability	struggle
to cling	independence	to predict	chore
to be employed	equal to	so far	role
to debate			

1. The *fight* for women's vote started in 1848 during a special convention held in Seneca Falls, in the state of New York.

2. Until then, women had no rights at all. They had to accept their function, which was limited to household *tasks* and *raising* children.

3. The husband was the only *moneymaker* in the family.

4. And if the wife *had a job,* by law the boss had to give her *payment* to her husband.

5. A married woman had no *personal freedom,* and nobody seemed to believe in her *skills.*

6. The convention organizer, Elizabeth Cady Stanton, maintained that women were *as good as* men and that they deserved the same rights, including the right to vote.

7. Her ideas, ridiculed at first, gathered a *growing* number of supporters after 1865.

8. They were, however, hotly *discussed*.

9. Newspapers proclaimed that most women were satisfied with the traditional *womanly* role.

10. New Zealand was the first country to give women the right to vote in 1893. Two states of the Union (Wyoming and Utah) had passed laws giving women the same rights in 1869, but the other states *held tightly* to the old ideas for a number of years.

11. The main reason was that the politicians were not *eager* to let women vote because they couldn't *tell in advance* how they would vote.

12. *Until now* women's vote has not made much difference. Women usually vote as they would if they were men with the same background and education.

Word Forms

Complete each of the following sentences with the correct word; be sure to make the necessary changes in the noun and verb forms.

1. *politics, politician, political, politically*

    a. Many women say that they are not interested in _____ .
    b. But women could play an important _____ role in their country.
    c. Do you think that they would be smart _____ ?
    d. _____ , they could be a great force.

2. *commuter, commuting, to commute*

    a. People who work in the city and have their home in the suburbs must _____ every day.
    b. Some _____ have to drive an hour each way.
    c. It may be difficult to find a job within _____ distance from the house.

3. *activity, active, actively/action, to act*

    a. Jenny is a very _____ person.
    b. She is _____ involved in her husband's business.
    c. But her many _____ didn't leave her much time to relax.
    d. We always admire her _____ .
    e. Peter often _____ in haste and without thinking.
    f. Many of his _____ are rather foolish.

4. *romance, romantic, romantically*

    a. It's spring; _____ is in the air.

    b. We saw a very _____ picture last night, about a young couple in love.

    c. This beautiful _____ was taking place in Italy.

    d. And the moon was shining _____ over them.

5. *to depend, dependent, independence, independent, independently*

    a. In the past, women have always been _____ on their parents, their husbands, or other male relatives.

    b. But they have gained more _____ now in most countries.

    c. If they can support themselves, they don't _____ on anyone when they are adults.

    d. Working allows them to live _____ .

    e. The colonies wanted to be _____ from the mother country.

6. *brightness, to brighten, bright, brightly*

    a. A _____ child is an intelligent child.

    b. If you'd paint the walls yellow, it would _____ the room.

    c. You can talk of the _____ of a room or of a child.

    d. The room might be _____ decorated.

    e. His face _____ when we gave him the good news.

7. *shyness, shy, shyly*

    a. He doesn't dare to ask for an explanation because he is too _____ .

    b. When one asks him a question, he answers _____ .

    c. With time he may lose some of his _____ .

8. *ignorance, to ignore, ignorant, ignorantly*

    a. He doesn't seem to know anything; we didn't think he was so _____ .

    b. When you are traveling you can make mistakes because of your _____ of the customs of the country.

    c. You may _____ do something very wrong.

    d. To say that a person is _____ of the rules of a game means that he doesn't know them.

    e. But if a person didn't *try* to follow the rules, you would say that he _____ them.

To Be Looking Forward To

Use the following suggestions to make a few sentences including *to be looking forward to,* as shown in the examples. Notice that in sentences like "He was looking forward to doing something," the verb is always in the *-ing* form.

Examples: He. A new job.
  He is looking forward to his new job.
  He was not looking forward to the new job.

  He. Work with father.
  He is not looking forward to __working__ with his father.
  Is he looking forward to __working__ with his father?

1. You. To go to London.

2. I. To meet your parents.

3. They. To find the results of women's vote.

4. You. To go to college next year.

5. I. To be among new people.

6. She. To live in the city.

7. She. To take care of her cousin's children.

8. The cousin. Her assistance.

9. He. To cook his own dinner.

10. They. New experiences.

Some /Any /No

Read the following sentences aloud, supplying either *some* (in affirmative statements), or *any* (in questions and negative statements), or *no* (for *not any*).

1. A journalist recently learned, with _____ surprise, that NASA was training six women astronauts.

2. "What kind of women," he wondered, "would have _____ desire to work in space?"

3. He went to NASA, asked to see the six, and spent _____ time with them.

4. He asked them first if there was _____ glamor *(charm, romance)* in being an astronaut.

5. "No, but plenty of hard work," they said. "It doesn't make _____ difference whether an astronaut is male or female. The training is the same."

6. They admitted that there could be _____ doubt in people's mind about women's ability to do the work.

7. "Women do have _____ difficulty with part of the training, due to the fact that they are smaller and lighter than men."

Parachute

8. "A fifty-pound parachute° on a one-hundred pound girl is sure to create _____ problems."

9. "But we always find _____ way to do our duty, in our own fashion."

10. The journalist asked whether women would have _____ special role in space.

11. "Not as women, but as specialists in _____ field, certainly."

12. Two of the women are doctors in medicine; four have Ph.D.'s in _____ useful science.

13. They are all good pilots. NASA didn't see _____ reason to excuse them from flying big planes.

14. "Was there _____ reason to train only male astronauts, until now?" the journalist asked.

15. "No," said a NASA official. "It has taken _____ time for us to seek female astronauts."

16. "But there were no females only because the first missions needed trained pilots, and there was _____ female pilot available."

17. "Now other skills are in demand; the program needs several geologists, for instance. And _____ of them can certainly be women."

18. "There is _____ reason to exclude them."

Sentence Combining: The Fact Is That

Change the sentences using the suggested phrase, as shown in the example.

Example: Women tend to marry later now. That's a fact.
          The fact is that women tend to marry later now.

1. Older women could not get jobs, a few years ago. That's a fact.

2. Employers preferred to hire younger persons. That's the truth.

3. They found that older women are good workers. That's the truth.

4. They are dependable and interested. That's a fact.

5. Now older women are in demand. That's the result.

6. There are more women doctors now. That's a fact.

7. Most women still don't study for good careers. That's the truth.

8. They believe that business degrees are for men. That's the trouble.

9. They think that sciences are for men. That's a fact.

10. They could be good mechanics or engineers. That's the truth.

11. Parents often discourage them from trying. That's one of the problems.

12. Men often resent women engineers. That's the trouble.

13. Most women become nurses or secretaries. That's the result.

14. Most women don't feel proud and self-confident. That's a fact.

Topics for Discussion or Composition

1. Is it better to get married early or late? What is the best age, in your opinion?

2. Should husband and wife share the household chores? Are there chores that a man can not or should not do?

3. Women are now working as truck or taxi drivers, miners, ship captains (in the Coast Guard), surgeons, and in fact in any profession they choose. Do you approve? Are there professions that shouldn't be open to women or that women can not do well?

4. What do you think of women in military academies?

5. Should women in the army or navy work only as clerks, drivers, nurses, or in other "safe" jobs, or should they be trained to fight?

6. Men are now taking on some professions that have always been reserved for women: nursing, teaching kindergarten children, secretarial work. Do you think that they can do these jobs as well as women? If you were in a hospital, would you like to have a male nurse?

7. Do you think that a woman who has children under the age of seven should stay at home or should go to work even if she doesn't need the salary?

8. Do you think that most women vote like their husbands? Do they influence their husbands' votes?

9. In your opinion, why do people divorce, in most cases?

10. Do men and women get married for the same reasons? If they don't, why do men marry and why do women marry?

For Composition Only

1. Make an outline of this essay, listing the main points and the supporting details.

2. Make two lists, based on this essay, of:
   a. the good effects of the new role of women
   b. the bad effects of the new role of women

14

The Right Message

ALTHOUGH HIS self-given title of "clothes consultant°" doesn't sound entirely serious, William Thourlby performs a valuable service for those who seek his advice. His customers are men on their way up* who wonder why they are not socially successful, or why they are not rising faster in their company. Suspecting some personal flaw°, they ask Thourlby to examine them and give his opinion. If the man's problem is a matter of improper clothing, it is promptly solved. Thourlby knows what to do. He knows it so well that he is often consulted by statesmen and politicians concerned with their public image*; and when the president wore a sweater for a televised interview, the White House asked Thourlby what he thought of this informal costume (he disapproved).

person who gives advice

imperfection

William Thourlby is surely familiar with* all the old sayings° such as "Clothes do not make the man" or "One shouldn't judge a book by its cover." But his experience has led him to doubt the truth of these well-known proverbs°. A former actor, Thourlby had often observed the difference that a costume could make in the appearance of the men and women acting with him in a play. A man who had arrived at the studio looking dull, common, or even ridiculous in ill-chosen clothes, would emerge from the dressing room like a man of authority: a judge, a doctor, a learned scientist, the perfect lawyer. Not only would he look different but he would move and walk in a manner befitting° the character. Because of his clothes, he *was* dignified, elegant, or brilliant. He *felt* different. This doesn't happen only to actors and actresses. Who has never felt transformed by a beautiful (or ugly) dress, by a new coat? A high-school student was asked recently what she thought of the fact that pretty clothes were in fashion again at her school. "It's a good change," she said. "It has helped me. When I dress up*, I feel energetic° and successful. I am happier, I work better. I feel good about myself."

ancient and famous statements

sayings

right for

full of energy

Eventually, Thourlby decided to give up acting and to make a career of helping people dress right for the part that they wanted to play in real life. The idea proved excellent. The "clothes consultant," who charges fifty dollars per hour, is kept busy flying all over the country for consultations. His customers seem to feel that he deserves his fee.

Thourlby was once called by an important businessman who wasn't really pleased with his own success. The man, who was dealing with heads of states, foreign ministers, and international bankers, thought that there was something wrong in the effect that he produced on them. He had noticed that his business acquaintances seldom invited him to their home. After looking at the man's large and expensive collection of clothes, Thourlby advised him to discard° most of them. All the splendid coats with colorful linings and gaudy° buttons, all the fancy shirts and showy ties had to go*. The businessman was also

throw or give away
too bright

persuaded to give up diamond rings and to replace his watch. Discreetly elegant, he resumed his career with new confidence, sure now that he was giving the right image of himself as a respectable, responsible, trustworthy individual.

Appearance, of course, is not just a matter of clothes; gestures, voice, the way a person moves and talks are just as important, because they reveal character. "When a man steps into a room," says Thourlby, "even if he is not known, people make ten decisions about him, based on his appearance. These decisions cover his wealth, his education, his family, his success, and his character." The judgment rests on° details: does the man wear a "serious" tie or a gaudy one? Are his shoes too pointed? Does he walk erect° and confident or is he humbly stooped°? Does he have a strong handshake? Does he laugh too much and talk too loudly? Does he look people in the eye? Does he eat properly? And so on.

Today's magazines carefully instruct their readers on the kind of clothes and manners that will help them get a job, find a mate°, and in general lead a successful life. Actually, who needs to be told that a gracious smile, a good coat, and plenty of self-confidence will get you better service in any store and a nicer table in a restaurant? All this advice about appearances angers the individualists who insist on* living and behaving as they please. They maintain that rules about dress are an unacceptable limitation of personal freedom. What right does an employer have, for example, to make his employees wear a certain type of coat or shave their beards? "Every right," thinks the employer, well aware that the public judges his business by the appearance of the people who work for it. William Thourlby is frequently invited to lecture to the personnel of large companies anxious to present a good conservative image. He takes along* an eccentric tie and a loud plaid jacket to illustrate the "wrong" way to dress for business. He usually sees many similar clothes in the audience.

Another complaint of the individualists is that it is unfair to "judge the book by its cover," or the man's intelligence and abilities by his looks. It is true that Albert Einstein[1] was not a picture of elegance* in his shapeless sweaters and baggy° pants; and his refusal to wear tie and socks ("useless nuisances," he said) never concealed his genius. But genius has its privileges, and Einstein never had to worry about people's opinion of him. Among ordinary beings, looks do mean something. While a man's costume doesn't say anything about his intelligence, it says plenty about his personality, about his judgment, and about the opinion that he has of himself. "If that man had any sense,"

rests . . . is based on

straight / *humbly . . .* bent forward like a humble person

husband or wife

shapeless, loose

[1] Albert Einstein (1879–1955) was a German-born physicist, and one of the great minds of all times. His work has transformed our understanding of matter, energy, time, and the universe.

reasons a possible employer, "wouldn't he try to look attractive enough to make me want to hire him? Is he too lazy to make the effort? In that case, what kind of a worker can he be? Does he feel so bad about himself, and could his judgment be correct? Perhaps he doesn't really want to work, or to be taken seriously. Is his appearance a sign of hostility° or arrogance°? Is he a troublemaker? Or is it just that he is, after all, stupid?"

unfriendliness, readiness to fight / feeling of superiority

    The same kind of question will come to the mind of anyone who sees a person wearing, by choice, the wrong kind of clothes for any occasion. The man who appears at a party or a reception in a not-too-clean plaid shirt, without tie, or at a business meeting with a two-days growth of beard will never be mistaken for an absent-minded° genius. People will assume that he is crude°, arrogant, or anxious to be "different" at all costs—or a desperate failure. Fairly or not, everyone reaches a decision about his personality and situation. If the decision is wrong, the man has nobody to blame but himself; he has delivered the wrong message.

thinking of something else
ill-mannered, rough

IDIOMS AND EXPRESSIONS*

Idiom	Definition
on their way up	successful in their careers, and expected to rise even farther
their public image	the way they appear to the public
to be familiar with	to know
dress up	put on formal or especially nice clothes
had to go	had to be discarded, abandoned
to insist on	to be determined to
to take along	to bring with
a picture of (elegance)	a good example of (elegance)

THE VOCABULARY OF CLOTHES AND APPEARANCE

A man's <u>suit</u> includes a <u>pair of pants</u> and a <u>coat</u> or <u>jacket</u>.

With the suit, a man wears a <u>shirt</u>, a <u>tie</u>, and perhaps a <u>sweater</u> if the weather is cold.

<u>Socks</u> and a pair of <u>shoes</u> complete the <u>costume</u>.

<u>Blue jeans</u>, the most popular type of pants,

are worn everywhere for informal occasions.

<u>Baggy</u> pants are too big and shapeless.

Thourlby says that it is best to wear <u>discreet clothes</u> that won't be noticed; coats shouldn't have bright <u>linings</u> (inside layer of the coat) and they shouldn't be made of gaudy plaid material.

Clothes are ill chosen, even if they are elegant, when they are not befitting (right for) the occasion.

The fashion is the style in favor at a particular time. To be discreetly dressed, one shouldn't be too fashionable.

A person's costume reveals (shows) something of the person's character.

It is just as revealing as the person's gestures (the motions of his body and of his hands).

One can tell some of a person's flaws and qualities by that person's looks (appearance) and manners.

A proud man walks erect with his head high.

A man can be stooped by age, or because he is humble or shy.

An arrogant man, who feels very superior, steps boldly into a room.

A consultant in any field is worth consulting because he is an expert.

EXERCISES

Understanding the Text

1. How would you describe William Thourlby's work?

2. Why is it interesting to mention his first career?

3. In what different ways are people transformed by their clothes?

4. Since Thourlby's customers are in important places, why are they consulting him?

5. What was wrong with the businessman's clothes in the fourth paragraph?

6. Why are clothes important in a person's life?

7. What advice would you give to a man or a woman going to a job interview?

8. Why are employers interested in their employees' appearance?

9. Are people judged only on their clothes?

10. Why is Albert Einstein mentioned in the essay?

11. Is it wise for an employer to refuse a job to a candidate who seems dirty and carelessly dressed? Why?

12. Why is it obvious that the importance of clothes is not an *American* discovery, nor a *new* one?

Vocabulary

1. The *absent-minded* student is not studying very well because:
   a. he does not understand what he is reading

    b. he is not thinking of what he is reading
    c. he is planning to miss the test anyway

2. When an idea has many *flaws:*
    a. it is not perfect
    b. it has many uses
    c. many people approve of it

3. It is *befitting* to wear jeans:
    a. at a cocktail party
    b. on a beach
    c. when meeting heads of states
    d. in bed

4. A man's *gestures* are:
    a. the clothes he has collected
    b. the movements he makes with his body
    c. the people with whom he does business
    d. his imperfections

5. A *ridiculous* story is:
    a. foolish
    b. false
    c. very amusing
    d. original

6. You *discard* something when:
    a. you throw it away
    b. you choose it
    c. you like it very much
    d. you keep it

7. Friends invite you for dinner and say, "*Don't dress up.*" They mean:
    a. don't wear warm clothes
    b. don't wear a heavy coat
    c. don't wear formal clothes

Word Forms

Complete each of the following sentences with the correct word; be sure to make the necessary changes in the noun and verb forms.

1. *consultation, consultant, to consult*

    a. Large businesses and organizations often _____ experts who know part of their operation particularly well.
    b. A retired engineer may be a _____ for the company he has left.

   c. He is called once in a while for a _____ on a problem that he knows well.

2. *suspicion, to suspect, suspicious, suspiciously*

   a. We felt very _____ when we saw that man enter the store.
   b. We had a _____ that he didn't want to be seen.
   c. He was acting _____ , touching the items on the shelves and keeping an eye on the saleslady.
   d. But she did not seem to _____ him at all.

3. *flaw, flawed, flawless, flawlessly*

   a. William Thourlby always dresses perfectly; his manners too are _____ .
   b. He was consulted by a wealthy man who would have been elegant if his appearance had not been _____ by a very gaudy tie.
   c. This was the only _____ in his costume.
   d. He gave up his ties and is now dressed _____ .

4. *familiarity, to familiarize, familiar, familiarly*

   a. Before going to a foreign country, you should _____ yourself with the culture of that country.
   b. It helps to have some _____ with the language.
   c. Thourlby has spent a great deal of time in London; he is _____ with the city.
   d. It was easy to see that they were good friends; they talked very _____ .

Idioms

A. Change the following sentences to express the same idea while using one of the idioms in the list. Be sure to make the necessary changes in the verbs.

to be familiar with	to insist on (doing)	to take along
to be a matter of	to keep from (doing)	

   1. Some people *are determined* to judge others by their appearance.

   2. They can make a mistake if *they don't know* the people's origins.

   3. Sometimes, manners *are related to* national customs.

   4. Don't forget to *take* your warmest coat *with you*.

   5. The man *was determined* to meet William Thourlby.

   6. He said that his problem *was not related to* clothes at all.

7. He said that his shyness *prevented him from* behaving well in society.

8. Since *he did not know* the customs of the city, he asked what he should do.

9. How can we *avoid* making the wrong impression?

10. Can we *take* the children *with us?*

B. Change the following sentences, using the idiom as shown in the example. Pay attention to the tense of the verb.

Example: I get up in the morning when *my mother* calls me.
My mother makes me get up in the morning.

1. Thourlby travels often because of *his new career.*

2. He flies to all kinds of places where *his clients* call him.

3. Jack lost his job because of *that beard.*

4. But he shaved his beard to please *his new wife.*

5. We laugh sometimes when we see *the new fashions.*

6. A woman feels more confident when she is wearing *good clothes.*

7. The president discarded his sweater for public appearances, because of *Thourlby.*

8. Sometimes we reach the wrong judgment because of *appearances.*

9. He looked ridiculous because he was wearing *ill-chosen clothes.*

10. The manager hesitated to hire the candidate because of *his bad manners.*

11. You will look thinner if you wear *dark clothes.*

12. Will you look thinner if you wear *dark clothes?*

13. Would you look thinner if you wore *dark clothes?*

14. You won't look thinner if you wear *dark clothes.*

Combining Sentences: A Written Composition Exercise

See how many different sentences you can create with the facts provided in each group of statements, by using words such as:

and	who	since	although
when	which	and since	but
where	that	but since	however
because			

Examples: Facts:
> Einstein was absorbed in his work.
> He found time to play his violin.
> He loved music.

Sentences:
> Although he was absorbed in his work, Einstein found time to play his violin, for he loved music.
> Einstein was absorbed in his work; he found time to play his violin, however, because he loved music.
> Einstein was absorbed in his work, but he loved music and found time to play his violin.

Facts:
> In 1933 Einstein went to America.
> He was fifty-four.
> He remained there until his death.

Sentences:
> In 1933, when he was fifty-four, Einstein went to America, where he remained until his death.
> Einstein went to America in 1933, when he was fifty-four, and he remained there until his death.

1. Albert Einstein was born in the city of Ulm, in Germany.
   He received most of his education in Switzerland.
   He also lived there as a young man.

2. At one time he lived in Munich.
   He was a small child then.
   His father had a business there.

3. Albert Einstein is one of the great geniuses of all times.
   He was not a good student as a child.
   He was going to a German school.

4. He said later that the school was too military.
   He didn't like anything military.
   He didn't pay attention to what was taught.

5. Einstein's father was having financial difficulties.
   He took his family to Italy.
   Albert was fifteen at the time.

6. Albert was delighted.
   Unfortunately he had to finish high school.
   He couldn't go with the rest of the family.

7. In 1905, Einstein published a scientific article.
   He was twenty-five years old.
   This article changed scientists' understanding of matter and energy.

8. In 1933, Einstein became professor of physics at Princeton.
   He lived there until his death.
   His death occurred in 1955.

Topics for Discussion or Composition

1. In your opinion, is it fair or unfair to judge people on their clothes and on their appearance?

2. Is this equally true in the different countries that you know?

3. What other factors help form an opinion about a person: speech, voice, walk, eating manners, handwriting, or any other revealing details? Which are the most important?

4. Does an employer have the right to tell his employees how to dress and look while at work?

5. Should schools have rules about clothes and appearance?

6. Do you judge a store or a restaurant on its appearance? What do you consider important?

7. Can you compare the way people behave when they meet or are introduced to each other in different countries? Compare greetings, handshakes, kisses, bows, and other customs.

8. Can you mention some gesture or behavior that is good manners in certain countries but not in others?

9. Have you been surprised by some American custom or behavior? If you have traveled, have you been surprised by some customs or behavior in other countries?

10. What proverbs do you know about clothes?

11. Look at the list of proverbs provided below; can you quote other proverbs on the same topics, or add some on different topics?

> Proverbs: Better is the enemy of Good.
> Familiarity breeds contempt.
> A stitch in time saves nine.
> Money is the root of all evil.
> Idleness is the root of all evil.

One should not look a gift horse in the mouth.
Where there is smoke there is fire.
A bad workman always blames his tools.
Actions speak louder than words.
A bird in the hand is worth two in the bush.

For Composition Only

1. If you are familiar with a country that is not the United States, describe briefly how people dress for different occasions, and describe what is *not* considered a good way to dress.

2. What differences have you noticed in the way people eat? Compare the way people eat in the United States and in the country where you have lived.

15

TO LIVE WITHOUT WORKING

T HE PRECEDING chapters have shown us what changes have occurred in people's ideas and values during the last two decades. Justice, patriotism, the role of women, and family life are not today what they used to be a generation ago. Through Sam and his son we are now going to observe what has happened to the notion that work is an important and noble duty.

*   *   *

Sam was a grocer in the Bronx.[1] All his life he had worked hard, first as the only employee in the same small grocery, and then as its owner. The store, which opened at 7:30 A.M., never closed before eight in the evening—and often later, for Sam never refused to serve late customers when he was still around cleaning up the place. His wife helped during most of the day, and her sister came in the morning to prepare the sandwiches that they would sell at noontime. Sam's three children had always been expected to give a hand* when they were not in school or doing their homework.

Sam took his long days as a matter of course°. Like most men of *matter . . .* normal thing
his age and modest background, he regarded work as the normal human fate. He didn't resent taking pains* to assure the financial security of his family because he was convinced that anything of value has to be earned. Surely, it never occurred to Sam* to wonder whether this security was costing him too much freedom and personal happiness. For one thing, he didn't consider himself unhappy or unfairly burdened. He was just a man doing his duty. Besides, he had his rewards: the store had prospered° nicely since he had bought it and he felt proud succeeded
of his success. It was good also to know that he had earned the respect and friendship of his neighbors; it was good to feel needed, responsible, and liked.

For Sam the little store didn't represent only a hard way to make a living* and to provide his sons with the education that he had not received himself. It was not just a place to work. It was his true home, his world, the very center of his life, and his pleasure as well. He enjoyed his daily conversations with his customers, the jokes he shared with the policeman on the beat*, and the company of Fred, the tailor next door, who came every day for an apple and a bit of gossip°. talk about news and people
During the quiet hours of mid-afternoon, Sam would stand at his door, between the oranges and the potatoes, happily surveying his street. He belonged there, in this community of shopkeepers who shared his problems and his satisfactions.

Sam's sons tried in vain to talk him into* retiring at seventy. He couldn't imagine a life away from his store, his responsibilities, his friends; the very idea of doing nothing made him uncomfortable. Sam ran his store until he was seventy-four. One morning, as he was carrying

---

[1] The Bronx is a part of New York City.

fell down

a box of apples outside, he collapsed° and died of his heart attack without having been sick or idle one day. That was pretty much what he had hoped for.

At the time of his father's death, Sam's youngest son George was thirty-eight years old. A geologist°, he held a demanding and highly paid position with a company that built nuclear reactors.[2] He had to explore possible locations for new reactors and to study the ground to see if it was safe. The job involved much traveling, but George didn't seem to mind° being away from his family for long periods of time, and spending evenings on paperwork° when he was back home. The resulting break-up of his marriage saddened him without bringing any change in his way of life. Anyone who knew George would have described him as a hard-working, ambitious, competitive° man with a splendid future in the company.

expert in soils and rocks

resent, be upset at
writing, reading for a job

eager to compete, to fight

Eleven months after his father's death, George stopped working. He was not fired; he was not pushed out by a rival; he simply quit. His friends could hardly believe the news at first. When they tried to get an explanation, George told them that, after much reflection, he had reached the conclusion that his beloved career was robbing him of his life. He had always been too busy to pay attention to anything that was not connected with his work; too busy to share the interests of his wife; too busy to see the days and the years go by°. In short, he had been nothing but a successful robot. Now he was going to stop running and take a good look at the world. He wanted to get to know himself, to watch the birds in his garden, and to become aware of the passage of time. No, he said, he had no intention of looking for another job after a while; and he had no desire to travel. He was just going to live and think in peace, at leisure.

go ... pass

the only one

George's case is not unique°. In the last fifteen or twenty years, quite a number of men and women have chosen to drop out of the working world to try a different kind of life. Most of them are in their thirties and forties, often well educated, although all ages and backgrounds can be found among them. A variety of reasons have led them to give up their work and the security it provided.

strain, overwork

Some, like George, have given up a career that was demanding too much from them. Others couldn't stand the pressure° and the competition. A thirty-five-year-old woman, who had a high position in her company, decided to leave when she found herself suffering from allergies[3] that made her life miserable. She had two children and no savings°; but even her anxiety about the future couldn't spoil her feeling of relief and her new peace of mind. Her health improved. She may

money saved for the future

[2] A nuclear reactor is a group of machines built to produce nuclear energy.
[3] An allergy is a condition caused by all sorts of substances (dust, bits of animal furs) or by great anxiety. The allergy can cause skin problems or breathing difficulties.

never work again; if she does, she says that she will take small
temporary° jobs.   *not long lasting*

Some people, on the contrary, have quit jobs that were boring or
meaningless to them. An office employee who has been pushing papers* for years may start wondering whether those papers are achieving
anything. An engineer in a large company, aware that he could be
replaced by any man with the same training, may come to feel unimportant as an individual. Such people leave their work in the hope of
finding stronger interests and a sense of personal worth.

There are also people who leave their work to fulfill an old dream,
such as writing books, painting, sailing to remote islands, or growing
fruit trees. An army officer left the service at thirty-eight to build doll
houses, and another one, who had always been interested in archae-
ology, did the same at forty-five to dig ancient Indian sites°; his wife   *places*
was delighted—instead of keeping house, she was going to satisfy her
own dream of learning to make paper.

But most of the men and women who drop out of the working
world have no special interest and no desire to take up* any occupation. They want only to enjoy their freedom, their independence, and
their leisure. No more rushing to catch a morning train, no more commuter traffic, no more anxiety to please a boss, no more meetings, no
more obligations to behave and dress according to the rules. This endless vacation does not necessarily bring happiness; many of those who
have chosen it as a style of life admit that leisure, too, can become
boring. But they still prefer it to their former existence. The main problem remains the lack of financial security for, with few exceptions, the
"dropouts" are not wealthy. And so they survive by selling their possessions, by borrowing from friends and family, and by taking an odd
job° now and then for a short time when it becomes absolutely nec-   *odd . . . small temporary*
essary.   *job*

Sam would never have understood their attitude. In the first place,
he had never been unhappy with his occupation, and he had never
felt any conflict between his work and his personal life. Neither had he
ever dreamed of doing anything but sell groceries and chat with Fred.
And there was yet another factor. Today's dropouts can always find
some small job to do when they are in need of money; or perhaps they
can get unemployment compensation[4] from the government for a
while. But Sam had lived through the 1930s, when work of any type
was almost impossible to find. In those days a job, no matter how
unpleasant or poorly paid, was a man's most precious possession. Losing it was a disaster; not looking for another one, a shame. As for* not
wanting to work at all, it was unthinkable, for society was not used to

---

[4] Unemployment compensation is money the government gives to help people who have
lost their jobs.

loafers then. A nonworking family man would have lost the respect of his friends and his place in the community of responsible men.

point . . . way of thinking

George might have tried to explain to his father the new point of view°, to tell him that people have a right to be free, independent, and to watch birds all day if they want to. He would not have convinced Sam, for whom independence and leisure were luxuries that had to be deserved through hard work. Sam himself had enjoyed a vacation once in a while, and he had been happy to rest in the sun without his tie. But that was only because, having earned his fun, he could enjoy it with a good conscience.

It would have shocked Sam to learn that those "shameless" people who choose to live in unearned idleness have a good conscience too.

IDIOMS AND EXPRESSIONS*

Idiom	Definition
to give a hand	to help
the children give a hand	*the children help*
to take pains	to make a great effort
he didn't resent taking pains	*he didn't resent making a great effort*
to occur to	to think of
it never occurred to Sam to wonder	*Sam never thought of wondering*
to make a living	to earn enough money to live on
policeman on the beat	policeman who walks regularly in the area; the *beat* is the route he follows
to talk him into	to persuade him to
his sons talked him into retiring	*his sons persuaded him to retire*
to push papers	to do useless paperwork
to take up	to start
to take up any occupation	*to start any new occupation*
as for	and concerning

THE VOCABULARY OF WORK AND LEISURE

Sam <u>made his living</u> (<u>earned</u> his money) by running a grocery.

His son, a <u>geologist</u>, had a demanding job.

There was much <u>pressure</u> and <u>competition</u> with his <u>rivals</u> in the company.

But George was <u>hard working</u> and <u>ambitious</u>.

His position was highly paid and George may
have been able to save money, and to
keep savings in a bank.

Odd jobs, which are temporary and easy to
do and require no training, are usually
poorly paid.

George did much paperwork at home: he
had reports to read and to write.

He had no time to relax or to take a vacation.

He decided to quit his job, although he was
too young to retire. He wanted to rest and
have fun.

George was not fired by his boss; in fact he
had a great future in the company if he had
remained in it.

Sam was a successful grocer. His grocery had
prospered.

The prosperity of the store was Sam's reward.

Sam disliked idleness. He only stopped
working when he collapsed (fell
exhausted). Working was Sam's way of life.

He had a good conscience (he felt right about
what he was doing) when he took a
vacation.

He felt that he had earned this luxury
(unnecessary pleasure or good).

From Sam's point of view, George should
have had a bad conscience. He should
have felt guilty.

When an office worker works on papers that
do not seem important, do not seem to
achieve anything, it is sometimes said that
the man is just "pushing papers."

EXERCISES

True or False?

When the statement is completely true or completely false, answer *yes* or *no*. If the
statement is only partly true, explain why in a few words.

1. Sam was a self-made man.

2. Sam worked hard because he wanted to be rich and leave his grocery.

3. Sam never had fun or vacations.

4. Sam was a good family man.

5. George was always lazy and uninterested in his job.

6. George's decision to stop working angered his father.

7. George didn't manage to be a good worker and a good husband at the same time.

8. Sam had the same problem.

9. Nowadays the people who stop working are those whose work is not interesting
enough.

10. More people can live without working nowadays because they have plenty of
money.

11. An idle man always loses the respect of his friends.

12. Sam and George thought differently because they had not had the same kind of youth.

13. The dropouts today want exactly what the young rebels of the 1960s wanted.

14. Sam would be glad to know that the dropouts live with a bad conscience.

15. A dropout is not always a person who wants to do nothing.

16. Some dropouts are bored with their idleness, but prefer not to work anyway.

17. Both Sam and George agreed that leisure was a luxury.

18. Sam had a good life.

Vocabulary

A. 1. If a medicine gives *temporary* relief to your headache:
   a. it relieves it partly
   b. it relieves it for a while
   c. it cures it completely
   d. it is dangerous

2. When an employee is *fired* from his job:
   a. he has been burnt on the job
   b. he is excited about his job
   c. he was shot while working
   d. he has lost his job

3. *"It's a matter of course"* means:
   a. it's normal
   b. it's a place for races
   c. it's a source of competition
   d. it's a topic for a paper

4. When psychologists say that "every man is *unique*," they mean:
   a. every man is lonely
   b. every man is different from the others
   c. every man is alone
   d. every man is like other men

5. *Commuter traffic* is:
   a. useless papers
   b. the mass of cars carrying people to work
   c. the time it takes a person to go to work
   d. a change of personnel

6. If a friend tells you "I am *allergic* to cats" (or "I have an allergy to cats"), you understand that:
   a. your friend should avoid being near cats
   b. your friend hates cats
   c. your friend loves cats
   d. your friend is an expert on cats

7. "I don't like George's *point of view*" means:
   a. I don't like the way he looks
   b. I don't like the way he dresses
   c. I don't like the way he thinks
   d. I don't like the place where he lives

B. 1. Can a policeman hurt someone with his *beat?*

2. Sometimes a car is a *luxury;* sometimes it is not. Can you explain the difference?

3. *Gossiping* is not considered a nice activity, usually. Can you guess why?

4. How do you make a *sandwich?* What kind of sandwiches do you like best?

5. Is there a difference between salaries and *savings?*

6. How did Fred *make his living?*

Word Forms

Complete each of the following sentences with the correct word; be sure to make the necessary changes in the noun and verb forms.

1. *conviction, to convince, convincing, convincingly*

   a. Sam had very strong _____ about a family man's duty.
   b. He _____ his sons that they had to go to college.
   c. He talked to them very _____ about the joys of hard work.
   d. He thought that his own happiness was a _____ proof that he was right.

2. *friendship, friend, to befriend (to treat as a friend), friendly*

   a. When Sam arrived in the Bronx, Fred _____ him.
   b. This was the beginning of a long _____ .
   c. The neighbors were surprised, for Fred was not a _____ man.
   d. He didn't have any _____ besides Sam.

3. *competition, competitor, to compete, competitive*

   a. George's brothers are not as _____ as he is.

b. "I couldn't stand the _____ he has to face in that company," says his older brother Jerry.

c. "I wouldn't like to _____ with him."

d. "He is a tough _____ ."

4. *attention, to pay attention, attentive, attentively*

a. Sam always listened _____ to what his sons were saying.

b. He heard their complaints with great _____ .

c. He _____ to their ideas and projects.

d. But he wanted them to be equally _____ when he was talking to them.

e. And he wanted them to be _____ to their studies.

5. *intention, to intend, intentional, intentionally*

a. Fred's son has been _____ avoiding his father.

b. Fred knows that his son's absence is _____ .

c. The son has the _____ of quitting school.

d. He _____ to talk to his father soon.

6. *misery, miserable, miserably*

a. When Fred was a child, his family had no money at all; they lived in great

_____ .

b. Fred is not poor any more; he doesn't live _____ .

c. But he suffers from a different kind of _____ ; he is very ill and feels _____ most of the time.

Idioms

Change each of the following sentences to express the same idea while using the proper idiom. Be sure to pay attention to the tense of the verb.

to occur to   to talk (someone) into   to give a hand to   to go by

1. George always *helped* his father in the store.

2. Whenever he appeared, his father said, *"Help me,* will you?"

3. As the years *passed,* Sam unsuccessfully tried *to persuade* George to become a grocer.

4. Sam *never thought* that George was tired of grocery work.

5. *Do you ever think* that geology is a very interesting field?

6. Few weeks *pass* without the newspapers mentioning geologists at work.

7. Perhaps I can *persuade* you to study geology.

8. George *never thinks of* calling his brothers.

9. Months *pass* without any communication between the brothers.

10. But Jerry told George, "I am moving and I'd like you *to help me.*"

11. He *persuaded* George to call their younger brother Paul.

12. Paul said, *"I'll help you,* Jerry."

13. George *has never thought of* talking to Fred.

14. Many years *have passed,* and Fred is very old.

15. He is still working but a young tailor is *helping him.*

16. And his wife has *persuaded* him to retire at the end of the year.

To Occur

Answer the following questions with a sentence including *it doesn't occur to . . .* or *it never occurs to. . . .*

A. Examples: Sam's wife doesn't make the sandwiches. Why?
It doesn't occur to her to make the sandwiches.

Sam's wife never makes the sandwiches.
It never occurs to her to make the sandwiches.

1. Fred doesn't come in the morning. Why?

2. He never takes a pear. Why?

3. He doesn't pay for his apple. Why?

4. Sam never asks for payment. Why?

5. Fred and Sam never sit down to chat. Why?

6. They don't take a walk together. Why?

7. Sam's wife never chats with them. Why?

8. Sam doesn't go to Fred's shop. Why?

B. Examples: Sam's wife didn't complain.
It didn't occur to her <u>to complain</u>.

Sam never knew that she was tired.
It never occurred to Sam <u>that she was tired</u>.

1. Sam never hired an employee.

2. His sons never thought of becoming grocers.

3. They didn't know that their mother was bored.

4. The parents never took a vacation.

5. Sam never thought that his wife wanted to travel.

6. She didn't think of telling him.

7. She didn't think of selling the store after his death.

8. The sons didn't think that she could sell it.

9. She didn't think of traveling alone.

10. She never thought that George could go with her.

11. George didn't think of marrying again.

12. His mother never thought that he wouldn't.

Past Conditional

The past conditional is used to describe an unreal situation in the past. Change the following sentences as shown in the examples, using the past perfect in the *if* part of the response, and the past conditional (*would have, could have*) in the other part.

Examples: George stopped traveling; his marriage lasted.
   If George had stopped traveling, his marriage would have lasted.

   He explained his problem; he could get a different job and he kept his wife.
   If he had explained his problem, he could have gotten a different job and he would have kept his wife.

1. Sam listened to his sons; he retired at seventy.

2. He sold his store; he moved to Florida.

3. His sons helped him; the work was lighter and he could keep his store.

4. He left the Bronx; he lost all his friends.

5. He went to Florida; he missed Fred very much.

6. He lived near the sea; he could fish all day.

7. He liked to fish; he was very happy.

8. He tried to play golf; his wife could play with him.

9. Sam and his wife were happy in Florida; they stayed there forever.

10. They were too bored; they went back to the Bronx.

11. The grocery was for sale; Sam could buy it back.

12. George was bored with his idleness; he came to give a hand.

Topics for Discussion

1. What do you think of George's decision: was it wise or foolish?

2. Would you like to live without working all your life, with or without money?

3. What do you think of the different types of dropouts mentioned in the text—those who quit working to be with their family, to think in peace, to do something else, to feel more important, to be less pressured?

4. What would you do with your time if you never had to work?

5. Do you like or dislike Sam? Why?

6. If you have lived in different countries, have you noticed differences in the way people work and live?

7. Small groceries like Sam's are rare now; they have been replaced by supermarkets. What is best? Where do you prefer to shop?

8. Do you know someone who is very bored with his or her work? What does he or she do? Why is it boring? Why does he or she do that work?

9. If you know a person who works very hard (too hard?), tell us about him or her. Is that person happy?

10. What would you prefer: too much work or not enough?

For Composition Only

1. Outline in two columns the differences between Sam and George, in background, life experience, and attitudes.

2. Make an outline showing the types of people who drop out of the working world and their reasons for doing so. Give supporting examples when possible.

3. If you know a man like Sam (a storekeeper, perhaps, or another modest worker), write a short description of the man, his work, and his life.

4. Write a paragraph in the past conditional tense, starting with: "If I had been one of Sam's sons, . . . "

16

A NEW ROLE FOR THE ZOO

ZOOS[1] HAVE EXISTED for so long that the first ones are lost in the darkness of the past. We know that in Iraq pigeons were kept in captivity as early as 4500 B.C., and that by 2500 B.C. India had herds° of half-tamed elephants. At that time, the Egyptians were hanging collars around the necks of their tamed antelopes°, and kept leopards°, monkeys°, and other creatures in their "animal farms." Most ancient rulers owned collections of animals; in 1000 B.C. the Chinese emperor Wen Wang installed his in a vast park that he named "the Garden of Intelligence."

large groups

Oryx antelope

Leopard   Monkey

Man's interest in wild creatures seems to have remained high at all times and in every part of the world. When the Spaniards entered the capital of Mexico in 1519, they found there a magnificent zoo where three hundred keepers were looking after* hundreds of birds, beasts, and snakes for the pleasure of their emperor. But after Wen Wang, the word "intelligence" was not often used in connection with animals. Until the eighteenth century A.D. even the kind people who took good care of their own pets°, even the best-informed thinkers remained convinced that animals had no soul, no understanding, no feelings, no capacity° to suffer. As a result, they did suffer a great deal, and still do. Most were kept in misery and solitude° in small cages; the luckier ones lived in elegant buildings near a king's palace. In either case more thought was given to the pleasure of the visitors than to the comfort of the captives.

animals living in the house

ability, capability
loneliness

The first "modern" zoo was established in Vienna, Austria, in 1752, and was promptly imitated in other countries. The zoos' only purpose at the time was to offer a new kind of entertainment to the public and to make money in the process*. But some scientifically-minded° individuals were beginning to be curious about the animals' anatomy°, their diseases, and their habits, although it was nearly impossible to judge their normal behavior under the conditions of their captivity. Even so*, knowledge spread; books were written, societies were formed to study or protect all animals with paws°, wings, or scales.

interested in science
body structure

animals' feet (with claws)

---

[1] A zoo is a place, generally a garden, in which captive (not free) animals are displayed to the public.

By the middle of the nineteenth century, many of today's great zoos were already in existence. They are still there—with many new ones—but both their appearance and their purpose have been thoroughly transformed.

The main reason for the changes was man's sudden realization that the wilderness was disappearing everywhere, and that animals were disappearing with it. Due to the human population explosion° and to merciless° hunting methods, many animal species have already been destroyed. There are no more wild Mongolian horses in Mongolia, no more Sumatran tigers in Sumatra, no more Hawaiian geese in Hawaii, no more oryx antelopes in the Arabian desert. Only a few of these animals survive in one zoo or another.

The modern zoological° park has become the last refuge° of vanishing species. It is true that the zoos themselves have contributed to the destruction of some species when they were all eager to get new animals from the wild for their collections. For every bird, zebra, or kangaroo that reached the zoo alive, many were killed during capture and many more died on their way to captivity. Many beasts still die of heat, thirst, or lack of air in the crates° where they are packed for transportation. In order to avoid such waste and suffering, the directors of the great zoos have stopped buying animals from dealers; instead, they breed their own animals, trade among themselves, or borrow the male or female that they need. Another change in the organization of the zoos has also been helpful: the parks do not try to show one specimen° of every animal species in existence; they exhibit fewer species, each represented by a group of animals living together in families or herds almost as they would in the wild.

A modern zoo is still a place where families can look at unfamiliar beasts, laugh at the monkeys, stare at the lions, or try to share their food with a haughty° camel. But the idea that the zoo will make money in the process of amusing the crowd had to be abandoned long ago. With its special buildings and grounds, temperature control, medical care, special foods and other expenses, a zoo is a very costly establishment. It can only survive if it receives funds from a zoological society, or from the city or the state in which it is located. Furthermore, unlike the zoological gardens of the past, a modern zoo is not run exclusively as a show. Its three main goals, as described by one of the most energetic directors, are: first, to study the animals; second, to assure their survival by breeding and protecting them; third, to educate the public and turn zoo visitors into animal lovers.

The study of animals in parks and in the wild has given a deeper knowledge of their habits; the result has been a great improvement in the way they are treated, housed, and bred. For example, most animals are now kept in groups because it has been discovered that, like people, they are happier in the company of their fellows. It has been recognized

population . . . rapid growth of population without pity

related to animals / place of safety

wooden boxes

example, individual

very proud, arrogant

also that as they are complicated creatures, keeping them happy enough to flourish° and multiply in captivity is a complicated operation. Zoo directors, keepers, and veterinarians° have countless stories to tell about the problems that have to be solved before romance can bloom in the zoo. Some animals won't breed without a special diet°; others must feel far from human presence, and others need large spaces for their courtship° dances. Some males insist on fighting to win their mate. Then there is the question of personal preferences, as was demonstrated by Chin-Chin, the female panda of the London Zoo, and An-An, the male panda in Moscow. After long and difficult discussions between representatives of the two countries involved, it was eventually decided that the two bears would take turns* flying to each other's residence in England and in the USSR. The humans went to considerable expense and trouble to get the bears together, but they couldn't get them interested in each other. It seems that all pandas are hard to please; the Washington Zoo has been struggling with its own pair for years, without much result.

 With most animals, however, the breeding programs, which are the second concern of zoos, work well enough to save vanishing species from complete extinction. The American buffalo, extremely rare thirty years ago, now counts forty thousand head, thanks to* the Bronx Zoo, which started breeding them. The oryx, extinct in its native Arabia, is doing so well in an Arizona park that it has been possible to send a herd back to its original desert.

 As for the education of the public—the third goal—it seems to be making good progress too. While zoologists° worry about the proper diet for giraffes and study the language of whales, the dances of bees, and the particular behavior of other beasts, crowds of visitors flock° to zoos to observe the animals. And now they don't always see the captives sitting sadly in cages too small for their size, for the presentation has changed a great deal. When their funds and their location allow it, most zoos try to install their collections in "natural" settings, with mountains and lakes, trees for the monkeys and flying space for the birds. Whenever possible, they mix the species as they would be in nature. The visitors can observe tigers swimming in their pool and lion cubs playing in the grass with their keeper—thus getting an idea of the way animals behave when they are free. In some very large parks the animals are truly free and it is the visitors who have to remain "caged" in their cars to visit them.

 There are still many bad zoos and many pitiful roadside exhibits of mistreated animals. Even a well-intentioned zoo director has serious problems with the eternal shortage of money and the lack of space for a zoo located in the heart of a big city. But most parks still try to fulfill their third duty of showing to the public, and particularly to children, the wonders of the animal world. Groups of school children are taken

remain very healthy

animal doctors

choice of food

the winning of a mate

students of animals

go in large numbers

set . . .   built, established

Penguins

through the zoo and all its buildings, and animals visit classrooms; children's parks are set up° to allow young humans to meet and pet furry and feathery babies. Some zoos have started an "adopt-an-animal" program: any person who contributes money to feed a particular snake, goat, fox, or penguin° can consider himself a "parent" of the animal. This doesn't give him much more than the right to visit the creature of his choice*, and the satisfaction to know that his donation helps in a small way. It can't be claimed that such contributions keep the zoos in operation, but the program does succeed in getting more people personally interested in the existence of the parks.

As men and beasts get used to each other, kindness and understanding may slowly develop on one side, trust on the other. Both sides would gain by it. "After all," says a zoo director, "the zoological garden is the only piece of 'wilderness' that most people will ever see; while it does much to protect the animals, it performs a valuable service for humanity itself."

IDIOMS AND EXPRESSIONS*

Idiom	Definition
to look after	to take care of
were looking after birds	*were taking care of birds*
in the process (of)	while; at the same time
in the process of amusing the crowd	*while amusing the crowd*
even so	however; although it is that way
to take turns	to go one after the other; to alternate
they would take turns flying	*one would fly one time, the other would fly the next time*
thanks to	due to
thanks to the Bronx Zoo	*due to the Bronx Zoo, because of the Bronx Zoo's efforts*
of his choice	chosen by him; that he has chosen
the creature of his choice	*the creature he has chosen*

THE VOCABULARY OF ANIMAL LIFE

A beast is any animal with four legs.

Cats, dogs, and other creatures with claws (animals' nails) do not have feet, but paws.

Cats have fur, birds are covered with feathers and fish with scales.

Therefore, a furry baby might be a lion's cub, and a feathery one might be a young pigeon.

Thousands of years ago, most animals were wild and free, until they were tamed by man.

Cats and dogs became pets, animals who live as friends in people's homes.

Snakes, birds, and other kinds of animals can be pets also.

Hunters hunt and kill animals, zoologists study them, and veterinarians ("vets") take care of them when they are sick, and generally look after them.

A vet might recommend a special diet for a sick animal.

Animals captured in the wild are packed in crates or cages and sent to the zoo that ordered them.

Modern zoos prefer to trade or breed their animals.

Some animals never breed in captivity, but others flourish in the zoo.

Some vanishing species have been saved from extinction by the great zoos' breeding programs.

There are now large herds of buffalos in America and a new herd of oryx antelopes in the Arabian desert.

Zoology students study the anatomy of animals, which is the structure of their body, the way their body is built.

EXERCISES

Understanding the Text

1. Why is a Chinese emperor mentioned in this article?

2. What do we know about the Mexican emperor's zoo?

3. Why did our ancestors treat animals so badly?

4. Are animals well treated now?

5. Why are people more concerned about animals now?

6. Could we say that man is responsible for the disappearance of some types of animals? Why?

7. What are the three goals of a modern zoo?

8. Are they different from the goals of the first zoos?

9. Why don't zoo directors buy their animals from dealers?

10. How do they get new animals?

11. Are zoos financially successful?

12. Why is it difficult to breed some animals?

13. What are the two big problems of today's zoos?

14. In what way is the display of animals different now from what it was in the old zoos?

15. Zoos are trying to make their animals live as "naturally" as possible. Can you give some examples of their efforts?

16. What is the difference between a zoologist and a vet?

Vocabulary

A. 1. Do the words *animal* and *beast* mean exactly the same thing?

2. A tiger is a cat; but is it a *pet?*

3. If you want a plant to *flourish,* what do you have to do?

4. People who are afraid of getting fat *go on a diet.* Does it mean that they go for a walk?

5. What is the difference between a *crate* and a *box?*

6. Why is the camel described as *haughty?*

B. 1. The *anatomy* of an animal or of a human being is:
   a. the country of origin
   b. the structure of the body
   c. the spirit
   d. the background

2. A mother is *looking after* her child when she:
   a. tries to find the child
   b. takes care of the child
   c. admires the child
   d. resembles the child

3. A *herd* of elephants is:
   a. a group of elephants
   b. a baby elephant
   c. a solitary elephant
   d. the place where an elephant lives in the wild

4. A *refuge* is:
   a. a "no" answer
   b. a display
   c. an animal's nail
   d. a place of safety

5. A *furry* animal is:
   a. afraid
   b. very angry
   c. covered with fur
   d. wild

Word Forms

Complete each of the following sentences with the correct word; be sure to make the necessary changes in the noun and verb forms.

1. *wilderness, wild, wildly*

   a. There are still untamed horses in the United States; they are beautiful and

   _____ .
   b. The poor animal was so frightened that it was running _____
   around its cage.
   c. Some people go to observe the animals in the African _____ .

2. *capture, to capture, captivity, captive*

   a. Lions and tigers live longer in _____ than they would in the wild.
   b. The _____ of a tiger is not an easy operation.
   c. It is always sad to see a _____ animal in a cage or a
   _____ man in a cell.
   d. They went to the South Pole and _____ a few penguins.

3. *capacity, capable, capably*

   a. Some zoologists are trying to find out if apes are _____ of communicating with human beings through sign language.
   b. The new director is running his zoo very _____ .
   c. Animals do not have the _____ to make sounds as humans do.

4. *mercy, merciful, mercifully/merciless, mercilessly*

   a. Tigers have been hunted _____ for their fur.
   b. The prisoner asked for _____ .
   c. The leader, who was in a _____ mood, let him go free.
   d. He never had treated his other prisoners so _____ .
   e. He was a cruel and _____ man.

5. *behavior, to behave, well behaved*

   a. Some visitors _____ very badly when they are in a zoo.
   b. You can be proud of your children's _____ .
   c. They are extremely _____ .

6. *protection, to protect, protective, protectively*

    a. A growing number of people are eager to _____ the remaining wild animals.

    b. Some are particularly interested in the _____ of whales.

    c. _____ laws have been passed in many countries.

    d. The lioness stood _____ in front of her cubs.

7. *destruction, to destroy, destructive*

    a. The most _____ creature is man.

    b. The spread of human population has caused the _____ of many animals' habitats.

    c. The fire has _____ several hundred acres of forest.

8. *satisfaction, to satisfy, satisfactory*

    a. In many small zoos, the conditions in which the animals live are not _____ .

    b. The birth of a rare animal is a source of great _____ to the zoo's vets.

    c. Will you _____ our curiosity and tell us what an oryx looks like?

Synonyms

Read the following sentences aloud, replacing each italicized word or expression with a word or expression from the list. Make all necessary changes in nouns and verbs.

furry	herd	magnificent	paw	captured
tame	capacity	to look after	pet	to pet
(in) solitude	cage	mercilessly	diet	vet (veterinarian)
refuge	dealer	specimen	species	to breed
pitiful	mistreated	shortage	set up	in charge of
keeper	crate	zoological		

1. The *animal doctor* of the Bronx Zoo, Dr. Emil Dolensek, is a very busy man.

2. Being *responsible for* one of the largest *animal (adj)* parks in the United States, he has *to take care of* thousands of *individual animals*.

3. The zoo is enormous and includes *large groups* of antelopes of all kinds, elephants, zebras, and other beasts.

4. It is a *safe place* for many *types of animals*.

5. First thing in the morning, the doctor takes care of the sick and performs operations. Then he rushes to the airport to look at two baby elephants waiting for him in their traveling *wooden boxes*.

6. They have not been recently *caught* and they were not sent by a *merchant*. They come from another zoo. But even when they have not been *badly treated*, animals can arrive in *very sad* condition if they have struggled in their boxes and hurt themselves.

7. Dr. Emil rushes back to the zoo for another operation. Then he has to welcome a group of young children; he takes them around to show them how his animal hospital has been *built;* then he takes them to the young animals' zoo, where they *gently stroke* the *fur-covered* rabbits and lambs.

8. Then he examines a mother gorilla who doesn't have enough milk; he orders a special *choice of food* for her.

9. He walks through the park, followed by a *friendly* guanaco from Peru, who seems to think that it is a *house animal* and a friend of the doctor.

10. Dr. Emil goes to the *box with bars* of a *gorgeous* Siberian tiger who always wants the doctor to scratch him behind the ears.

11. The doctor loves this particular cat, who seems to have a great *ability* for affection. The animal is alone in its cage, for tigers prefer to live *alone*.

12. Dr. Emil examines the tiger's *foot* because the *man who takes care of the animals* said that it was swollen (increased in size).

13. Siberian tigers have been hunted *without mercy* and there are not many left. But they *have young* easily in captivity.

14. The doctor goes back to his office, where there is no *lack* of work for him.

Prepositions

Read the following sentences aloud, supplying the missing preposition.

about	around	between	in	to
after	at	by	of	with
against	before	from	on	

1. Mohini died _____ old age in 1979; the keepers who looked _____ her are still mourning her death.

2. Mohini was the white tigress given _____ India to the population of the United States.

3. There were a number of meetings _____ the officials _____ the two countries _____ Mohini started her journey.

4. She was packed _____ a large traveling crate, and the director of the Washington Zoo, her future home, insisted _____ escorting her all the way.

5. Since white tigers are rare and beautiful, the public was very interested _____ Mohini when she arrived _____ the zoo.

6. Thousands of visitors came _____ the zoo to look _____ her.

7. Many would have loved to share a hamburger _____ her or to put their arms _____ her gorgeous neck.

8. Mohini had several cubs; great crowds came to see them play _____ the grass _____ their mother's tail.

9. They laughed _____ the cubs, and stared _____ Mohini with respect and admiration.

10. Big cats like tigers and lions live longer _____ captivity than they would _____ nature.

11. Mohini lived to be twenty years old, five years older than she would have lived _____ the wilderness _____ her Indian forests.

12. When she started losing weight, the keepers who were taking care _____ her noticed the change in her appearance and began to worry _____ her health.

13. The vet was ready to protect her _____ disease, but nothing could be done to save Mohini _____ old age.

14. The zoo director, who mourns Mohini as much as anyone else _____ the zoo, said, "If Mohini had been human, she would surely have been a movie star."

Indirect Speech

Remember how to use tenses in indirect speech:

Direct speech		Indirect speech	
	"I work"		he *worked*
He says	"I worked"	He said that	he *had worked*
	"I shall work"		he *would work*

After reading the following text through, retell it, line by line, in the form of indirect speech.

ROOM NINE GOES TO THE ZOO

Examples:	The teacher of Room 9 said, "*I have* a surprise for you."	The teacher said that *she had* a surprise for us.
	She said, "*You will not work* today."	She said that *we would not work* today.

"*You worked* very hard all week."	She said *that we had worked* very hard all week.

1. The teacher announced, "The class is going to the zoo."
   The teacher . . .
2. She explained, "The zoo is on the other side of town."
   She explained . . .
3. "We will have to take the bus."
   She said . . .
4. Angel said, "I don't want to go to the zoo."
   Angel said . . .
5. "I have been there a million times, and it's boring."
   He said . . .
6. The teacher said, "I am sorry but we'll go anyway."
   The teacher . . .
7. "I am sure that Angel will find it interesting this time."
   She said . . .
8. She said, "You can take your lunch in a paper bag."
   She said . . .
9. "We cannot bring food for the animals, however."
   She said . . .
10. "We will not be allowed to feed them."
    She said . . .
11. "The animals need a special diet, which an expert chose for them."
    She said . . .
12. "The wrong food can kill an animal or make it sick."
    She said . . .
13. "Something like that happened last week."
    She said . . .
14. "First we will visit the polar bears."
    She said . . .
15. Angel said, "I have seen the polar bears before."
    Angel said . . .
16. "They are lots of fun and I like them."
    He said . . .
17. The teacher told us, "Man is the only animal who can kill polar bears."
    The teacher told us . . .
18. Angel said, "I think that the animals are safer in the zoo."
    Angel said . . .
19. Another student said, "The animals are happier in the wild, even if they live a shorter life."
    Another student said . . .
20. Angel said, "I don't agree, but I will ask the bears."
    Angel said . . .
21. But Angel's little brother was not interested in the bears. He said, "We forgot to bring our lunch."
    Angel's little brother said . . .

Sentence Combining: A Written Composition Exercise

Turn each of the following groups of statements into one logical sentence, by using one or several of the following words:

who	when	although	since	in order to
that	where	but	because	
which	after (doing)	and	for	

Sometimes, several different sentences can be created, all correct. You may change the order of the facts provided when necessary to make a new sentence.

Example: Facts:
                 Gerald Durrell was born in India.
                 He didn't live there very long.
                 His family was British.
                 His family went back to England.
                 Gerald was five years old at the time.

                 Sentences:
                 Although Gerald Durrell was born in India, he didn't live there very long,
                 for his family, which was British, went back to England when Gerald was
                 five years old.
                 Gerald Durrell was born in India, but he didn't live there very long because
                 his family, which was British, went back to England when Gerald was five
                 years old.

1. The Durrells stayed in England a short time.
   They went to the island of Corfu.
   They lived there for several years.

2. Gerald had several brothers and one sister.
   He didn't play with them.
   He had better things to do.

3. Gerald made his family miserable (very unhappy).
   He brought home all sorts of animals.
   He kept the animals in the garage or in the living room.

4. Gerald didn't have any money.
   He was determined to set up an excellent zoo.
   The animals would be happy there.

5. Gerald finished his studies in France, Switzerland, and Greece.
   He decided to go to work.
   He wanted to make money.

6. He was not a zoologist.
   He had no experience with large animals.
   He got a job as student-keeper in a great zoo.

7. Student-keepers don't make much money.
   Gerald decided to do another type of work.
   The other type of work would pay better.

8. He spent many years in Africa and South America.
   He collected rare animals.
   He sent the animals to several great zoos.

9. Gerald Durrell writes very well.
   He also made money with books.
   He wrote the books about his adventures.

10. He had enough money.
    He bought a piece of land on the island of Jersey.
    He started organizing his zoo.

11. Gerald Durrell is very famous now.
    Many people go to Jersey.
    The people want to see him and his zoo.
    They have read his books.

Topics for Discussion

1. Do you like to go to the zoo? Why?

2. When you go to a zoo, which animals do you particularly like to watch? Why?

3. Have you visited a zoo that was particularly good or particularly bad? Why was it good or bad?

4. Which animals make the best pets?

5. Do you think that animals have feelings, intelligence, and memory?

6. Would you like to become a zoo keeper or a veterinarian? Why?

7. Some people hunt for food or to protect themselves. Some hunt for fun with guns. Some hunt for fun with cars, airplanes, or helicopters. Do you approve or disapprove of hunting in general, or in some cases? What do you think of fishing?

8. Rare animals are killed for their furs or their horns. What could be done to protect them:
   Forbid all hunting and trapping (catching animals in steel traps)?
   Severely punish hunters and trappers? How?
   Forbid the sale of furs and skins?
   Forbid women to wear fur coats? Make women who wear fur coats pay a fine?
   Allow all hunting but try to keep some survivors in zoos?
   Can you think of any other solutions?

9. Is it better for a wild animal to be in a good zoo or to be in the wild?

10. In general do you think that zoos are a good or a bad thing? Are they worth the money they cost?

11. Some zoos are not very good because they don't have enough funds. What could be done to help them financially? What would you suggest?

For Composition Only

1. Describe man's attitude towards animals from ancient times until today, in a short essay including introduction, body, and conclusion. Do not try to write about zoos.

2. Compare the zoos of the eighteenth and nineteenth centuries to modern zoos, including facts about the zoos themselves, the animals, and the purpose of zoological parks, and any other aspect that you can think of.

3. Which is your favorite animal? Why?

17

A Good Education

TWO FRIENDS—two women of European origin—were talking about education, or rather about the kind of education that they had received in their youth.

"I was very proud of myself when I finished college," said one. "I had received a classical education[1] and I had been very happy with the system. At that time, students were not allowed to select their own courses; but even if I had been consulted°, I would have chosen the subjects of the school's program. I liked history and literature; I was interested in languages and past civilizations, in philosophy° and music; and even in some sciences, although I was not very good in that field. I probably complained about the amount of homework; everyone did. But I enjoyed my studies and I felt that they were preparing me for life. I was very shocked, after graduating, when I discovered that I—the good student—couldn't get a job. My degree would get me into a university for further studies, but it couldn't help me find work, because I had no useful skill that would interest an employer. I have done well for myself since then, but it was not easy to get started."

asked

study of truth, wisdom

Her friend laughed. "You don't know how lucky you are," she said. "I was sixteen when I left school, and I went to work right away* in the accounting department° of a big factory. I had received in my school all the training I needed for my job, including bookkeeping, commercial arithmetic°, and typing. But I had never learned anything that was not absolutely practical. I had never heard of ancient civilizations and ancient languages. I did not know anything about music, and I would not have recognized the names of the most famous painters of my own country, whom everybody else seems to know. I had never discussed or even read a book of any importance; I did not know what "philosophy" was. And this is why, at forty, I am going back to school. I realize now that I have missed something important, something that would make my life fuller, that would give me great pleasure. I am going to make up for* it. I am going to get a good education at last."

accounting . . . section handling business accounts

use of numbers

Between them, these two women illustrate° clearly a question that has been debated for some time, and which has not yet received an answer acceptable to all: "What is a good education?"

give an example of

*   *   *

What is a good education? Is it one that covers as much as possible of human history and achievements, past and present? Or one that gives graduates the ability to find employment promptly when they leave school? Is it a broad education or a specialized one? Should it provide students with a vast collection of facts, or merely train them to

[1] Classical education, liberal education, traditional education: the three names are applied to the type of education that provides a broad general culture, as opposed to a scientific or technical training preparing students for a profession or a trade. Liberal education consists of the study of the "humanities": literature, languages, history and geography, philosophy, art, music, and other similar subjects.

222

think? Should a future engineer gain only the knowledge that will enable him to do his job properly, or would a richer background improve his professional ability as well as his personal life? The debate goes on and on*, with good arguments on both sides.

In the eighteenth and the nineteenth centuries, the question was not even worth asking. A good education was, *of course,* a broad one based on the humanities. An educated man knew "something about everything." He was familiar with the great deeds and the great ideas of the past. He had read extensively°; he was able to use his own language correctly and often elegantly. He could join in any conversation about plants, planets, painters, or politics. He was at ease in the world, and he knew that his education would open to him any career that he might want to try. Even if he was mostly interested in literature, he had some knowledge of the sciences and the techniques of his time.

widely, much

But sciences and techniques have changed a great deal since the latter part of the nineteenth century; and the world has changed too. It has become more complex and increasingly specialized. There is much more to know in every field. It is not only the scientist and the physician who need a long special training now, but the administrator°, the computer expert, the accountant, and the business manager. Besides, the multiplication° of college graduates has made the competition for jobs much harder than it used to be. The best qualified, the expert, wins.

manager

increase in number

American students started in the late 1930s to protest that college was not preparing them for the "real" world, the working world. They complained that they were getting too much useless knowledge and not enough practical, up-to-date° information in their chosen field. By the end of the 1950s, the protests had become very loud. "Latin and art appreciation are fine subjects for rich people who will spend their lives traveling and visiting museums," the students would say. "But we are in school to get prepared for a career, a job. We have to learn a mass of facts in our own field; why should we waste time on luxuries like music or Victorian poetry, unless we are planning to become musicians or professors of literature? Why force a future dentist to struggle with French grammar, or a future businessman to know who Tolstoy was? What good is* Greek philosophy to an engineer? The humanities have no value on the job market, and therefore they have no value for us."

current, of the day

Not only did the students ask for changes in the list of required[2] subjects, but they also demanded the right to choose their courses according to their own taste and future needs. No more established

[2] In order to graduate, students had to pass a certain number of "required" courses, plus some courses that they could choose from a list. For a long time, history, literature, and foreign languages courses were required.

programs, no guidance from educators° and professors. All they wanted · experts in education
was to get their degree as fast as possible and go to work.

Although the educators didn't all agree, a majority recognized that
times had indeed changed and that education should perhaps adapt
itself to the realities° of modern society. Colleges and universities · facts
revised° their programs to include a large number of specialized · changed
courses in business, nursing, engineering, and other professional fields.
In the 1960s they also added courses requested by the students be-
cause they considered them "relevant°" (Women's Studies, Revolu- · related (to something)
tion, or Black History) or useful (glass blowing°, infant care, jogging°, · glass . . . making glass/
or family life). The students were granted the right to choose their · slow running
courses as they wished. Many traditional subjects had to be dropped,
including history and foreign languages; the liberal education courses
that were still available were often neglected by the students, who didn't
feel like* working hard to learn something that was not required for
graduation.

Whether the revised programs have helped college graduates to
find employment promptly is not clear. But after fifteen or twenty years
of experimentation, they have raised a lot of criticism. Some of it comes
from the graduates themselves, who discover that their practical knowl-
edge is neither deep nor flexible°. As soon as they progress to higher · able to fit various needs
positions, they find that they need management training and more
study in their own field. Besides, they feel handicapped by their lack
of general knowledge; for example, by their ignorance of the language
and culture of the foreigners with whom they are doing business. Most
of all they suffer from their inability to use English, their own language,
easily and properly.

For their part, the employers complain that they see too many
"experts" who cannot write a simple report, analyze° a problem, think · examine the different parts
logically°, and defend or even present their own ideas. "Besides," say · of/with order and reason
the employers, "the ideas they do have are neither broad nor bold.
They seem unable to see a situation 'from above' in a mature° way. · fully developed
And, perhaps because of a lack of self-confidence, they are not willing
to take responsibility, to take charge of operations. They are followers,
not leaders."

The supporters of traditional education are not surprised. They
have always maintained that maturity of thought could only be gained
by the study of past thinkers and past events. In their view only a
thorough intellectual training can give a person the ability to look at
contemporary problems "from above," in a sophisticated° way. They · complex
remind the complainers that the purpose of a college education is to
enrich and train the mind; it has never been to help graduates get a
beginner's job. Just as military academies are not trying to train lieu-
tenants but future generals, the colleges were established to produce
future leaders, directors, ambassadors, and thinkers. And, they add,

this broad education was flexible because it was never limited to a narrow "speciality"; it could open many doors. They give as an example the British professor of philosophy who, at the beginning of the Second World War, became Permanent Secretary of the Ministry of Supplies—head of the war production industries of his country. He did a good job, not because he knew much about war industries at first, but because he had a well-trained mind, ready to reason and to handle any problem with confidence.

What is a good education? The question is far from answered. Once more, colleges and universities are revising their programs: they drop "fun courses" and reestablish some of the traditional subjects neglected since the 1960s. Many great schools are again requiring the students to take a number of classes in English, history, literature, the social sciences, philosophy, the natural sciences, and art if they want to get a degree. Meanwhile, the experts are trying to define the "good education" of our time. Obviously the purely vocational° training once favored is not enough. But neither is the gentleman's education of the nineteenth century. Educational programs must meet the demands of a modern world where men and women have to work and to deal with enormous problems.

related to a trade

What, then, is a good education at the end of the twentieth century? Some educators suggest that it should include foreign languages and the study of foreign cultures; a mastery° of English, including the ability to write and speak well, because communications have become all-important in the modern world, and also because "a person who doesn't speak and write clearly doesn't reason clearly either"; some knowledge of the social sciences (sociology, psychology) that deal with human relations and human problems; some basic knowledge of modern science, which would enable future voters to be better informed about current problems like nuclear energy. Finally, many educators insist that all college graduates should be familiar with computers and modern information systems, since the educated professionals of tomorrow will have to understand their machines. Is that all? "No, of course not," answer the educators. "We have not mentioned the two great building blocks of education: history and literature!"

perfect knowledge

*   *   *

Is this truly the best modern education? Perhaps. But every educator would add or subtract a few subjects. And no matter what list of courses would be offered, it would not be approved by all. Not only do the professors have their own ideas on the matter, but the students have theirs too. "I don't believe," protested a Harvard[3] student when his university revised its programs, "I don't believe that colleges have the right to define what an educated person is." But then, who has?

[3] Harvard, the oldest university in the United States and one of the most prestigious, was opened to its first students in 1638.

IDIOMS AND EXPRESSIONS*

Idiom	**Definition**

right away

to make up for

to go on and on

what good is . . .?

what good is it?

to feel like doing something

immediately, right now

to compensate for

to continue forever

how useful is . . .?

what is it useful for? of what use is it?

to want to, to be in the mood to do
   something

didn't feel like working

didn't want to work

I don't feel like studying today

*I am not in the mood to study today; I
   don't feel any desire to study today*

THE VOCABULARY OF EDUCATION

Educators are the experts who try to find the
   best methods of education, including the
   best list of courses to offer as a program to
   the students.

A student gets one or several credits every
   time he passes (succeeds in) a course.

In his third year in a college, a student
   chooses the subject in which he wants to
   specialize: this is his major. A student can
   major in philosophy, biology, or art, for
   example.

He graduates (receives his degree) when he
   has collected the proper number of credits.

Schools teach many subjects. Vocational
   schools teach trades, such as carpentry,
   accounting, bookkeeping (keeping business
   accounts), and typing. Those are practical
   subjects.

Colleges teach some subjects known as the
   humanities, including literature, history,
   and the arts.

They also teach the different sciences,
   including social sciences.

Philosophy is the study of problems such as
the meaning of human existence and ideas.

Scientists and technicians need to have a very
   up-to-date (very new) knowledge in their
   field, or specialty.

Students want to take courses related to their
   goal and to their needs. They say that such
   courses are "relevant."

A student of geology may say that the study
   of Spanish is "irrelevant" (not relevant) to
   his needs.

A person with literary interests is one who
   likes literature (writings in fiction, poetry,
   and drama).

A flexible education is one that can be used
   for various aims. A flexible wire can bend
   in any direction.

Education is expected to give maturity (the
   fullest mental development) and
   sophistication (complex reasoning).

To think logically is to think with reason and
   order.

To analyze a problem is to study separately
   all the elements of the problem. To analyze
   water is to determine its separate elements.

EXERCISES

Understanding the Text

1. Which of the two women had a practical education, the first one or the second one?

2. Were they good or bad students?

3. What was wrong with the first woman's education?

4. What was wrong with the second woman's education?

5. In the past, did an educated man know "everything"?

6. Why was he "at ease in the world"?

7. Why is it different now?

8. Why did students complain about their education after the late 1930s?

9. Why did students reject subjects like music or foreign literature?

10. What else did they demand, besides a change of program?

11. What was the reaction of the colleges?

12. Who criticizes the new system of education?

13. What are the main problems, according to the critics?

14. Have the revised programs helped the students to get jobs?

15. Why do some educators compare colleges to military academies?

16. What happened to the British professor of philosophy?

17. What does this example show?

18. Does the author conclude that the best education is the liberal education of the past century?

19. Are new subjects suggested for the education of the twentieth century?

20. Does everyone agree?

Vocabulary

1. A *bookkeeper*:
   a. works in a library
   b. repairs old books
   c. sells books in a bookstore
   d. keeps business accounts

2. *Philosophy* is concerned with:
   a. health
   b. the appreciation of literature and art
   c. the meaning of life
   d. elegant writing

3. If you write *extensively,* you write:
   a. very much
   b. very fast
   c. in large letters
   d. very slowly

4. An *administrator:*
   a. sells goods in a store
   b. teaches college courses
   c. manages an office or a company
   d. is head of a church

5. When you want to *jog,* you need:
   a. a ball and a friend
   b. a ball and a group of people
   c. a pair of comfortable shoes
   d. a swimming pool

6. "This argument is not *relevant* to our discussion" means:
   a. it has no relation to our discussion
   b. it has already been mentioned
   c. it is not intelligent
   d. it was not presented at the time of our discussion

7. If a person says, "I am very *flexible,*" he means:
   a. I am very interested
   b. I am stubborn
   c. I am well prepared
   d. I am willing to adapt to the circumstances

Word Forms

Complete each of the following sentences with the correct word; be sure to make the necessary changes in the noun and verb forms.

1. *enjoyment, to enjoy, enjoyable*

   a. We spent a very _____ afternoon.
   b. We _____ the new exhibit very much.
   c. The explanations of the artists themselves added to our _____ .

2. *management, manager, to manage, managed*

    a. I would like to speak to the person who _____ this office.
    b. The _____ is not here today.
    c. The shoe factory is very well _____ .
    d. There has been a change in its _____ .

3. *typist, typewriter, typing, to type, typed*

    a. Phillip has bought a new _____ .
    b. He is not a very good _____ .
    c. _____ is not difficult.
    d. He says that everyone should learn how _____ .
    e. _____ papers and letters are easier to read.

4. *knowledge, to know, knowledgeable, knowledgeably*

    a. The general public, he says, should _____ more about nuclear reactors.
    b. They need to have some _____ of their dangers and possibilities.
    c. They could make a decision _____ .
    d. Because they would be more _____ on the subject.

5. *skill, skillful, skilled, skillfully*

    a. This problem has to be handled _____ .
    b. Typing is a very useful _____ to have when you want to find a job.
    c. She sews well; she is very _____ with her hands.
    d. This job will require _____ workers.

6. *account, accounting, accountant, to count*

    a. We should keep a careful _____ of our expenses.
    b. Phillip is studying to become an _____ .
    c. It is strange that he should study _____ .
    d. When he was a child it seemed that he would never learn how _____ .

7. *speciality, specialist, to specialize, special, especially*

    a. She is teaching a _____ class for advanced students.
    b. Her _____ is Spanish literature.
    c. She _____ in the literature of the sixteenth century.
    d. Her husband is a _____ in children's diseases.
    e. All their children are bright, _____ the youngest one.

8. *maturity, to mature, mature*

    a. Peter is very _____ for his age.
    b. Some people seem to reach _____ earlier than others.

   c. He knows vaguely what he wants to do; but it will take some time for his plans
      to _____ completely.

9. *extent, to extend, extensive, extensively*

   a. We were impressed by the _____ of his knowledge.
   b. He has traveled _____ .
   c. He has gained an _____ knowledge of African history.
   d. The garden _____ as far as the river.

Idioms

Change the following statements to express the same idea while using the suggested
idiom. Be sure to pay attention to the tense of the verb.

A. *To make up for* (to compensate, to pay for)

   Example: How can I *compensate for* my mistake?
               How can I make up for my mistake?

   1. I couldn't come to work last week; I am *compensating for* the lost time this
      week.

   2. Whoever broke those windows must *pay for* the damage.

   3. She was not pretty, but her intelligence *compensated for* her lack of beauty.

   4. If you can't take the test, you'll *compensate for* it by writing an essay.

   5. He spent the last years of his life *compensating for* his bad deeds.

   6. The house is too small; but the view *compensates for* the lack of space.

B. *To feel like* (*doing*) (to be in the mood for, to wish)

   Example: We *were in the mood to* go out last night.
               We felt like going out last night.

              I'd rather not go out; I *am not in the mood for* it.
              I'd rather not go out; I don't feel like it.

   1. *I am not in the mood to* go to class this morning.

   2. *Do you wish to* learn glass blowing?

   3. They *wished to* ask a question but they didn't dare.

   4. When you *are in the mood for* it, write your thoughts on the question.

5. I just *am not in the mood to* jog early in the morning.

6. One day they will *wish to* read about the past.

7. Have you ever *wished to* start a new life somewhere else?

8. We don't *wish to* have lunch yet.

To Be Worth It

One can say: It is worth ten dollars./It's not worth that much.

It's worth it./It's not worth it.

It's worth doing./It's not worth trying.

Give your own answer to the following questions, using *worth* any way you want, as you would do in a conversation.

Example: Is a college education too expensive?
No, it's worth it.
Yes, but it's worth the expense.
It's not worth spending so much money on it.

1. Would you spend one hundred fifty dollars to buy a camera?

2. Would you study ancient Greek for four years?

3. Do you think that everyone should learn to type in college?

4. Do you think that mankind should spend millions to explore space?

5. Was it a good idea to send that recorded message on the Voyagers?

6. Are judges right to try new types of sentences?

7. Were people foolish to wait in line to see *Star Wars* and *The Empire Strikes Back?*

8. Do you think that a job-seeker should take the trouble to prepare what he or she wants to say before going to a job interview?

9. Would you pay fifty dollars an hour for William Thourlby's advice?

10. Some colleges offer a literature course on science-fiction novels. Would you take it?

11. Was it right to stop a dam costing more that one hundred thirteen million dollars in order to save that fish?

12. Shall we do this exercise all over again?

Emphasis: It's . . . Who

The construction *it is . . . who* or *it is . . . that* is used frequently when one wants to insist on a particular fact or to correct a misunderstanding:

> *It's a degree* that they want, not an education.
> *It's my mother who* teaches in that school (it's not my aunt who teaches there).
> *It was in 1977 that* she started teaching (not in 1978).
> *It was not in that school that* she started (it was somewhere else).

Respond to each of the following statements with a sentence including *it's . . . who (that)* or *it was . . . who (that)* to stress the part of the statement that is italicized. Remember that *who* is used to represent a person who is the subject of the verb, while *that* is used in all other cases. The part of the statement in parentheses may be left out of your response.

1. *Adriana* was educated in Holland in the 1960s.
   Adriana was educated *in Holland* (in the 1960s).
   Adriana was educated (in Holland) *in the 1960s.*

2. *Adriana* didn't want to learn bookkeeping.
   Adriana didn't want to learn *bookkeeping.*

3. I am supposed to meet *the manager* (in this office at two o'clock).
   I am supposed to meet the manager *in this office* (at two o'clock).
   I am supposed to meet the manager (in this office) *at two o'clock.*

4. The *Latin class* wasn't cancelled last year.
   The Latin class wasn't cancelled *last year.*

5. *The employers* are complaining about those poorly educated experts.
   The employers are complaining *about those poorly educated experts.*

6. *Roger* graduated from Harvard in 1978.
   Roger graduated *from Harvard* (in 1978).
   Roger graduated (from Harvard) *in 1978.*
   Roger didn't graduate from Harvard in 1978.
   Roger didn't graduate *from Harvard* in 1978.
   Roger didn't graduate from Harvard *in 1978.*

Topics for Discussion or Composition

1. Do you think that everyone should go to college? If not, who should?

2. What kind of education do you want for yourself: a practical one, or a more extensive one? What would you rather *not* study?

3. Should colleges offer "fun" courses like glass blowing, jogging, or flying? Should they offer "practical" courses such as home repairs, photography, and carpentry, or leave such subjects to vocational schools?

4. Who should choose the list of courses that a college student must take to graduate: the educators, or the students themselves?

5. Do you think that it is useless to study past history and past civilizations?

6. What is your favorite subject?

7. How could we describe a *modern* educated person?

8. An educator suggests a course in ethics (moral philosophy) for college students. What do you think of the idea? Who should teach ethics: colleges, all schools, families, or religious leaders?

9. If you are familiar with the education system of a country other than the United States, explain what is different in the school organization, the students, the teachers, and the methods.

10. Should students of both sexes receive the same education?

For Composition Only

1. Taking your facts from the essay, sum up the good points and the bad points of:
   a. liberal education
   b. overspecialized education

2. What do you like and dislike in American education as you know it?

3. If you know a country that is very different from the United States, describe who is considered an educated person there.

NUCLEAR ENERGY: PROS AND CONS*

18

I N MARCH 1980 SWEDISH VOTERS were called to the polls° to let their
government know how they felt about their country's nuclear[1] program. Sweden, which must import oil for seventy percent of its energy needs, had six reactors in service* at the time and six more
under construction*. The Swedes were being asked whether they
wanted these completed, or preferred to stop them and close the other
ones progressively over the next ten years. Did they want to go on
using nuclear power? The answer was "Yes." By a large majority, the
Swedes declared themselves in favor of the program.

voting places

Their vote had been watched closely by the population of other
nations where reactors have become a center of bitter controversy°.
The supporters of nuclear energy praised the Swedes' response as a
victory of reason over emotion. In their view, atomic energy offers the
only chance of survival of our civilization. The opponents, however,
think that it is the most direct way to extinction. Each side keeps quoting
its favorite scientists and engineers, all knowledgeable, all sincere—and
all disagreeing completely about the merits° and the dangers of nuclear
reactors. The general public follows the dispute, very confused and
very scared.

argument

good points, qualities

The opponents' main argument is that reactors are much too dangerous to be used at all. They point out that there have been several
accidents already, and that more can be expected in the future. A
severe earthquake, a fire in the plant°, a mechanical failure, a simple
human error might cause a release of radiation that would spread death
over a large area. Even without such disasters, a well-functioning reactor leaks small amounts of radiation and so might, in the long run*,
cause cancer and birth defects in the population. It would also affect
the surroundings, for the hot wastes warm up the water of rivers and
lakes, killing plants and fish. Finally, the opponents remind the public
that a nation that owns nuclear reactors also owns the means of building
nuclear weapons. And what if* terrorists° were to capture a reactor or
to steal some uranium?

factory

people who use terror to reach their goals

Why run such frightful risks, they conclude, since reactors are not
even necessary? All the energy needs of the world can be satisfied by
other sources, such as oil, coal, natural gas, solar heat, the wind, the
ocean tides, and even the burning of garbage and other wastes. There
is already one tide-activated plant in service in France; in Germany and
North America a few towns already get their electricity from waste-
burning installations in their suburbs. In the United States, solar energy
partially heats five thousand houses or so, and it could be used on a

[1] Nuclear energy (atomic energy) is produced by the fission (breaking apart) of the central
part (nucleus) of the atoms of a white, heavy metal called uranium. Uranium, like all
radioactive substances, sends out (radiates) energy—it sends rays of energy, or *radiation.*

larger scale*. The reserves of gas and coal are still enormous, and oil itself is not exhausted. Surely humanity can get sufficient power from all those sources until science finds a way of producing artificial fuels°.

substances producing heat or energy when burned

Actually, the opponents add, the best solution to the energy shortage is conservation of the natural fuels that are still available. Oil should be reserved exclusively for cars, and all car owners should learn to use their automobiles sparingly°. They could share rides to work, and walk as much as possible. It would really be no great sacrifice for each individual to reduce his consumption of fuel: less heat in the house, less cooling from the air conditioner in summer, fewer appliances°—and the problem would be solved.

rarely, in small amounts

machines like washing machines or vacuum cleaners

The supporters of atomic power shake their heads in disbelief; they agree that conservation might help in a limited way, but how many people would make the necessary sacrifices forever? Most would be unwilling to try, particularly since a large number don't even believe that there is an energy shortage.

They answer the critics' arguments. Oil, they explain, will be totally exhausted in another twenty years. Its price, already very high, will keep growing with the ever increasing needs of the world's population and with the decreasing reserves. In the meantime, since most great industrial nations must import their oil, their supplies remain at the mercy of* international crises°, terrorism, and other disturbances°; the risk of war between competing countries is ever present.

severe, dangerous periods / troubles

The reserves of gas, not completely known at the present time, may be as large as the reactors' critics believe, but they won't be available for use in the near future. As for the various other sources of energy (sun, wind, and tides), they are indeed interesting to explore, but extremely expensive and of limited use because the power that they produce is not transportable° over long distances, and must therefore be used locally.

is . . . cannot be carried

Coal is very abundant, particularly in the United States, where the known reserves would be sufficient to satisfy the country's needs for over a century. But coal is expensive (due to the cost of labor and transportation), dangerous to mine (one hundred miners die each year and thousands suffer from lung disease), and dirty to burn. It pollutes the air so badly that, according to the scientists, a massive use of coal would create a blanket around the earth and bring about a disastrous change in the climate of the planet.

What then? All this, announce the supporters of the atom, brings us back to nuclear energy, and to the conclusion that it is the key to the future. Nuclear energy is nonpolluting, inexhaustible, independent from foreign pressures and—yes!—it is the safest of all energy sources, because it is the most closely watched. The well-publicized risks, they say, have been greatly exaggerated°. It should be remembered that none of the past accidents have killed or even injured one single person

made to seem greater

and that, as a matter of fact, no death has been caused by a reactor since the nuclear industry started twenty-five years ago. The chances of dying from radiation from a nuclear plant are much smaller than the chances of being the victim of a traffic accident, of drowning, or of dying of cancer caused by smoke from other people's cigarettes. The danger of explosion doesn't exist at all, because a reactor cannot build up enough energy to explode like a bomb. As for the danger of accidents, the supporters add, it is extremely small: reactors are built to resist earthquakes much stronger than any earthquake ever known to man, and their operations are automatically stopped at the first tremor°.   shaking
At all times a number of safety devices are ready to replace any damaged mechanism; if a system should break down, the next one would automatically come into action.

While extremists on both sides shout slogans, the moderates tend to agree that all the possible sources of energy will eventually be developed and that nuclear energy will play its part. The great question, therefore, is to make it absolutely safe—and to convince people that it is.

The safety of reactors could be improved in many ways, say the experts. The sites of new plants must be chosen always with the greatest care; the construction of nuclear plants and the quality of their equipment must be controlled carefully by specialists, and the operation of reactors must also be watched by experts from a government agency rather than by the private utility companies° that built them. The per-   utility . . . companies
sonnel must be well educated about the operation of their reactor and   producing and selling
trained to deal with malfunctions°.   electricity
                                        mechanical failures

The greatest source of worry at the moment is the disposal of radioactive wastes. Until now these wastes have been packed in containers and buried in remote areas or dumped° in the ocean. The critics   dropped
of nuclear energy point out, wisely, that the containers, being neither leak-proof° nor strong enough to resist the pressure of the deep sea,   certain not to leak
will surely leak sooner or later, pollute the sea, and eventually poison the whole planet. They insist on the fact that the wastes remain radioactive for twenty-four thousand years, and that no method has been found yet to bury them safely or to neutralize° them. As could be   make safe
expected, the supporters of nuclear energy do not agree: their scientists explain that the long-lasting radioactive substances in the wastes are not dangerous, because their radiation is produced at a slow rate—they wouldn't hurt a man more than the radiation that he normally receives from space every day of his life. And they remark cheerfully that, while the danger of nuclear wastes lasts *only* twenty-four thousand years, ordinary poisons such as arsenic° never lose their power at all.   a violent poison

Over twenty methods of neutralizing nuclear wastes are already known; one of them, which has been tried in Europe, consists of turning the waste into a sort of glass that can be buried safely in water or soil.

Unfortunately, it is extremely costly and can't be used on a large scale*
until a way is found to reduce the expense.

The debate about nuclear energy is likely to continue for a long
time. Most European nations have chosen to follow the nuclear route;
they are building not only ordinary reactors but a few more expensive
"breeder reactors"—a type of reactor that produces more energy than
it consumes. In other countries, the fears of the public have slowed the
development of nuclear plants. In the United States, where the opposition is strong and well organized, seventy reactors are now in service,
producing about thirteen percent of the country's electricity (four percent of its total energy).

While the opponents protest "No Nukes!" the supporters continue
to insist that there is no alternative, that the question is not whether or
not we should use atomic power, but *how much* we should develop
it. "It would be foolish," they say, "to let ignorance and fear stand in
the way*; let's remember the people who wanted to stop the construction of the first railroad, claiming that it would be the end of mankind—
the human body was simply not built to withstand speeds of fifteen or
twenty miles per hour."

IDIOMS AND EXPRESSIONS*

Idiom	Definition
pros and cons	reasons for and against
in service	being used
under construction	in the process of being built
in the long run	over a long period of time
what if . . .?	what would happen if . . .? suppose . . .?
what if terrorists were to capture a nuclear reactor?	*what would happen if terrorists captured a nuclear reactor?*
what if it were to explode?	*suppose it were to explode?*
on a large(r) scale	in large(r) amounts
to be at the mercy of	to depend entirely on
it is at the mercy of international crises	*it depends entirely on international crises*
to stand in the way	to try to stop or delay

THE VOCABULARY OF NUCLEAR ENERGY

Matter is formed of atoms, and each atom possesses a central part or nucleus. The fission (breaking apart) of atoms produces nuclear or atomic energy.

The metal uranium (like radium and plutonium) emits (sends out) radiation or rays of energy that can go through almost any substance, except a few such as the metal lead.

Uranium, radium, and plutonium are radioactive metals.

Nuclear energy is produced and controlled in large and complex buildings called reactors.

A reactor functions (works) well as long as there is no malfunction, no mechanical failure.

It must be leak-proof (built to have no leaks).

Wastes are the substances left after the use of the uranium.

Oil, coal, gas, and all other substances that produce heat or energy by burning are fuels.

Utility companies provide electricity and power to the population, usually by burning oil or coal.

Since the reserves of fuels are diminishing, these companies encourage their consumers to reduce their consumption of electricity.

They tell them to conserve energy by having fewer appliances. Washing machines, electric stoves, vacuum cleaners, and electric can openers are appliances.

The nations that have no oil in their own soil import it (buy it) from countries that have plenty to export (sell).

A situation (or a disease) reaches a crisis (plural: crises) when it reaches a particularly severe and dangerous period.

THE VOCABULARY OF VOTING

Voters are asked to go to the polls now and then to express their opinion on a certain question.

If the question is very controversial (very likely to cause disputes), the supporters and the opponents discuss the pros and cons (the reasons for and against) with passion.

The controversy (dispute) sometimes goes on for a long time, with many debates and discussions.

Voters also go to the polls to elect (choose) their officials among the candidates who have been campaigning (competing) for positions. Each elector puts his choice on a ballot (election card or paper).

In an election, the majority wins; the minority loses.

EXERCISES

Understanding the Text

1. Did the Swedes have a good reason to vote as they did?

2. Why were other nations interested in their vote?

3. Are scientists and engineers for or against nuclear energy?

4. According to the opponents of nuclear energy, why is a well-functioning reactor dangerous?

5. Why are the hot wastes of the reactors dangerous to the environment?

6. The opponents of nuclear energy say that reactors are unnecessary. Why?

7. What is the main problem with the use of solar energy, wind, and tides?

8. What is wrong with the idea of conserving energy?

9. What is the problem with coal: a short supply?

10. Have nuclear reactors killed many people so far?

11. How long has nuclear industry been operating?

12. Why are people so afraid of nuclear wastes?

13. What has been done with the wastes until now?

14. Is there any other solution to the problem? Why is it not used?

15. In the United States, who builds and operates the reactors?

16. What is a breeder reactor?

17. Does it seem that reactors will be the only source of energy in the future?

Vocabulary

A. 1. When you are talking about the *merits* of a solution, you are talking about:
   a. its good points
   b. its bad points
   c. its applications
   d. its dangers

2. Which one of the following substances is not a *fuel?*
   a. coal
   b. wood
   c. water
   d. oil

3. A substance is not *transportable* when:
   a. it cannot be changed into energy
   b. it cannot be burned
   c. it cannot be carried over a distance
   d. it cannot be made safe

4. The risks are *exaggerated* when they are:
   a. hidden from the public
   b. small enough to be ignored
   c. carefully controlled
   d. described as greater than they really are

5. A *crisis* is:
   a. a poison
   b. a dangerous period
   c. part of an atom
   d. a small quantity of energy

6. The fuel used in nuclear reactors is:
   a. nucleus
   b. uranium
   c. lead
   d. gas

B. 1. Suppose that you read in the newspapers, "We all go to the polls Monday." What does it mean?

2. Would you like your financial resources to be *inexhaustible?* Why?

3. What can you do with *arsenic?*

4. If an apartment is described as *soundproof,* is it likely to be pleasant to live in? Why?

5. Is it ridiculous to say that garbage and trash are *fuels?*

6. Is it very dangerous to eat *sparingly?*

Word Forms

Complete each of the following sentences with the correct word; be sure to make the necessary changes in the noun and verb forms.

1. *reason, to reason, reasonable, reasonably*

   a. Man is said to be superior to animals because he can _____ .
   b. Should a wise man obey his heart or his _____ ?
   c. Some of the arguments are extreme and not at all _____ .
   d. It is very difficult for the extremists on both sides to discuss the question _____ .

2. *to spare, spare, sparingly*

   a. Could you _____ an hour to do some reading?
   b. The prisoner thanked his captor for _____ his life.

   c. We don't have much wood left for the fire; we'll have to use it
     _____ .

   d. There are two rooms on the first floor, and a _____ (*extra, not used*) room for guests on the second floor.

3. *terror, terrorist, terrorism, to terrorize, terrifying, terrified*

   a. In that horror film, a monster from space _____ the population of New York City.

   b. A person who threatens to blow up a plane or a city if his demands are not satisfied is a _____ .

   c. He uses _____ to get what he wants.

   d. _____ have killed many people in the past years.

   e. The people were _____ by the violence of the earthquake.

   f. It was a _____ experience.

4. *transportation, to transport, transportable, portable*

   a. Enormous flat boats called tankers _____ oil from continent to continent.

   b. The cost of _____ is getting higher all the time.

   c. People carry their _____ (*easy to carry*) radios in the streets, on the beach, and anywhere they go.

   d. Some goods are too heavy or too fragile to be _____ .

5. *conclusion, to conclude, conclusive, conclusively*

   a. After reading all the articles, we _____ that the opponents were wrong.

   b. Be sure to examine all the arguments before reaching a _____ .

   c. They have shown _____ that the new method could work.

   d. I don't think that the demonstration was _____ ; it does leave some doubts.

6. *consumer, consumption, to consume*

   a. We bought a new automobile; it will _____ less gas than the old one.

   b. Anybody who buys goods and services is a _____ .

   c. Many nations are trying to reduce their _____ of oil and other natural resources.

7. *explosion, to explode, explosive*

   a. Bombs _____ , but a person can also _____ with anger.

   b. Trucks carrying _____ substances are marked to warn everyone of the danger.

   c. He gets mad easily; he has a very _____ temper.

   d. The noise of the _____ was heard for miles.

8. *disposal, to dispose of, disposable*

    a. There is no way to _____ nuclear wastes other than to bury them.

    b. Instead of selling their product in glass bottles, they are now offering it in _____ containers that can be thrown away.

    c. The main problem of nuclear energy is the _____ of wastes.

Less/Fewer

Less and *fewer* have the same meaning, but *less* is used with singular nouns (*heat, wind*) and *fewer* with plural nouns (*cars, appliances, people*). Answer the following questions with a sentence including either *less* or *fewer*.

Example: Do small cars use more gasoline than large ones?
          No, they use less gasoline.

1. Does Sweden produce more oil than Saudi Arabia?

2. Do reactors kill more people than traffic accidents do?

3. Do the opponents want more reactors in the future?

4. Do ordinary reactors produce more energy than they consume?

5. Do they need more money to build an ordinary reactor than to build a breeder?

6. Are the Europeans building more breeder reactors than ordinary reactors?

7. Are there more fish in the Little Tennessee River now that the dam is built?

8. Do the Swedes show more fear of reactors than the American opponents do?

9. Will there be more oil in the world twenty years from now?

10. Should people smoke more cigarettes to remain in good health?

11. Do reactors have more accidents than coal mines?

12. Should we try to use more energy?

A Review of Idioms and Expressions

Read the following sentences, replacing each phrase in parentheses with the proper expression from the list.

as for	at the mercy of	due to	more or less
at leisure	on a large scale	far from	right away

under construction   in character   in haste   in theory
what if   in charge of   in mind (to have)   in the long run
in awe   in demand   in service   in the process of

1. _____ (supposedly), oil can be extracted from—taken out of—a rock called shale.

2. _____ (because of) its cost, it has not been done _____ (in great quantities) yet.

3. Some engineers are now _____ (working at) trying to find a cheaper way to make the extraction.

4. The operation is _____ (not at all) simple and requires much water.

5. It may prove extremely helpful _____ (over a long period of time), but the men _____ (who direct) the research say that we must be patient.

6. As long as there are no artificial fuels, oil will remain _____ (much desired).

7. Most people are _____ (impressed and afraid) of nuclear energy, because when they hear of atoms they _____ (think of) bombs, radiation, and explosions.

8. All humans feel _____ (about) the same on that subject.

9. A supporter of nuclear energy says, "The opponents are too emotional; they do not get enough information and so they reach their conclusions _____ (too fast)."

10. "They want all nuclear plants shut down _____ (immediately)."

11. "In some eastern states, where nuclear plants have been _____ (used) for years, they supply about fifty percent of all electricity."

12. "If the plants were closed suddenly, those eastern states would be without light and heat, and their industries _____ (about) stopped."

13. "Let's hope that the government considers the problem _____ (without haste)."

14. The Japanese can build a nuclear plant in nine to twelve years; the French in about ten years. _____ (and concerning) the Canadians, they can build one in about seven years.

15. There are several breeder reactors _____ (being built) in Western Europe.

16. "We are _____ (not at all) happy about the multiplication of reactors," say the opponents of nuclear energy. "_____ (suppose) some mad men took control of a small reactor somewhere. Millions of lives would be _____ (in their hands). And it would be _____ (like) for such people to get the ransom and let the radiation out anyway."

Combining Sentences: A Written Composition Exercise

See how many different sentences you can create with the facts provided in each group of statements, by using words such as:

and	who	because	although	besides
therefore	which	since	but	
however	that			

Example: Facts:
Coal is not a good source of energy.
It is expensive to produce.
It is dangerous to mine.
The reserves are enormous.

Sentences:
Although the reserves are enormous, coal is not a perfect source of energy because it is expensive to produce and dangerous to mine.
Coal, being expensive to produce and dangerous to mine, is not a perfect source of energy; the reserves, however, are enormous.
Coal, which is expensive to produce and dangerous to mine, is not a perfect source of energy; but the reserves are enormous.
Although the reserves are enormous, coal is not a perfect source of energy because it is expensive to produce; besides, it is dangerous to mine.
Since it is expensive to produce and dangerous to mine, coal is not a perfect source of energy, but the reserves are enormous.
Coal is expensive to produce and dangerous to mine; therefore it is not a perfect source of energy although the reserves are enormous.

1. Sweden has no oil for its industry.
   Sweden had to find other sources of energy.

2. The Swedes don't really like reactors.
   They voted for the nuclear program.
   The program would be good for their industry.

3. Nuclear power seems to be the energy of the future.
   There are other sources to explore.

4. Oil can be extracted from a rock.
   The rock is called *shale*.
   It is not a good source.
   The extraction uses a lot of water.

5. The production of shale oil is costly.
   The oil produced would be expensive.

6. Solar heat is an attractive source of energy.
   It is very clean.
   It is rather costly.
   It cannot be used all year round in most places.

7. Electric automobiles were built eighty years ago.
   They are clean and silent.
   People preferred gasoline automobiles.

8. Electric automobiles were slow.
   They didn't appeal to people.
   People wanted to drive fast and to go far.

9. They could not go far with an electric car.
   An electric car runs on batteries.
   Batteries didn't last long.

10. A new type of battery has been invented.
    It may be soon on the market.
    It will solve the problem.
    It can move a car at fifty-five miles per hour for one hundred miles.

11. Gasoline has become expensive.
    People are getting interested in electric cars.
    The electric car makes life more pleasant.
    It reduces noise in the street.
    It doesn't pollute the air.

Topics for Discussion or Composition

1. Together, let's review what the opponents of nuclear energy say:
   about the dangers of nuclear reactors—what can happen?
   about the dangers of the reactors without accidents
   about the need for nuclear reactors
   about the value of conservation

   How do the supporters of nuclear energy answer these arguments?

2. Are you for or against nuclear reactors? Why?

3. Why do you think the Swedes voted as they did?

4. Smoking is known to cause lung cancer, not only in the people who smoke, but in those who breathe the smoke from other people's cigarettes.
   Why do people keep smoking anyway?
   Should they be discouraged in some way (perhaps by high taxes on cigarettes)?
   Should they be forbidden to smoke in public places (such as stores, restaurants, streets, schools, or libraries)?

Should there be lectures on the subject of smoking to inform school students? Do you have any other suggestions?

5. Do you think that the public knows enough about the dangers and the merits of nuclear energy? Should they be better informed? How?

6. Do you think that the public should be asked to make a decision about the nuclear program of the country (as happened in Sweden), or would it be wiser to leave the decision to the government?

7. Do you think that science is going too far?

For Composition Only

1. Make an outline describing the different sources of energy available, and their pros and cons.

2. In two lists, outline the positions of the supporters and the opponents of nuclear energy, presenting the objection of one group and the answer of the other on the same line.

> The opponents say: The supporters say:
> 1. _____   1. _____
> 2. _____   2. _____

3. Explain your own opinion about nuclear energy in a short essay with an introduction, body, and conclusion.

Word List

The following list includes all the words that have been defined in marginal glosses or in the Vocabulary or Idioms sections of each chapter. Each word is accompanied by the number of the page where it appears and then by the number of the paragraph in which it can be found or by the following notations: *Voc* (Vocabulary), *I* (Idioms), or *F* (footnote). The first lines of a page are always counted as paragraph 1, even if they are only part of the last paragraph of the preceding page. Whenever necessary, words are identifed as noun (*n*), verb (*v*), or adjective (*adj*). The notations *sing* and *pl* indicate that the word is always used in the singular or the plural.

A

abandon 111-1
about
   how about? 86-I
   what about? 86-I
absent-minded 182-2
academic 60-1
according to 46-I
accounting department 222-3
act 112-Voc
activity 169-Voc
administrator 223-3
advanced 42-2
advancement 141-Voc
agent
   travel agent 4-Voc
album 29-1
alert *adj* 152-3
alert *v* 110-5
alien 43-4
allergy 193-F
along with 43-2
alternative 127-Voc
analyze 224-4
anatomy 206-3
ancestor 72-F
anchorman 138-1
anxiety 84-3
anxious to 60-2
apart
   tell apart 112-I
apologize 29-2
applaud 87-Voc
appliance 237-2
applicant 139-4
appointed time 152-2
appointment
   make an appointment
     154-Voc

approval
   win the approval of 86-I
archaeologist 4-Voc
archaeology 4-Voc
arithmetic 222-3
arrogance 182-1
arsenic 238-4
as for 195-I
aside
   set aside 169-I
aspiring 152-4
asset 153-3
assistance 124-2
astronaut 46-Voc
asylum 31-Voc
athlete 98-2
atom 240-Voc
atomic energy 240-Voc
attention
   bring to the attention of 4-I
   come to the attention
     of 112-I
   pay attention to 4-I
attorney 138-3
audience 87-Voc
average 141-Voc
awareness 168-1
awe
   in awe 2-1

B

baby-sit 16-4
bacteria 112-F
baggy 181-4
ballot 240-Voc
band 47-Voc
barrel 111-3
beast 210-Voc
beat

on the beat 195-I
befitting 180-2
bent on 126-I
better
   for better or worse 4-I
   we'd better 4-I
biography 98-4
blowing
   glass-blowing 224-2
board meeting 60-1
bookkeeping 226-Voc
brag 153-4
brakes *pl* 16-8
brand-new 60-1
breed *n* 72-4
breed *v* 111-4
bring
   bring about 30-I
   bring out 100-I

C

cancel 139-4
candidate 154-V
capacity 206-2
captive 206-F
care
   take care of 30-I
carve 30-Voc
case 111-1
celebration 31-Voc
celebrity 101-Voc
chant 46-Voc
character 87-Voc
   in character 100-I
charge
   in charge of 18-I